Good Housekeeping
Cookery Club

THAI

Louise Pickford

EBURY PRESS
LONDON

First published 1995

1 3 5 7 9 10 8 6 4 2

Text and Photography © Ebury Press 1995

First published in the United Kingdom in 1995 by Ebury Press,
Random House, 20 Vauxhall Bridge Road, London SW1V 2SA

Random House Australia (Pty) Limited
20 Alfred Street, Milsons Point, Sydney,
New South Wales 2061, Australia

Random House New Zealand Limited
18 Poland Road, Glenfield,
Auckland 10, New Zealand

Random House South Africa (Pty) Limited
PO Box 337, Bergvlei, South Africa

Random House UK Limited Reg. No. 954009

A CIP catalogue record for this book is available from the
British Library.

Managing Editor: JANET ILLSLEY
Design: SARA KIDD
Special Photography: GUS FILGATE
Food Stylist: LOUISE PICKFORD
Photographic Stylist: PENNY MARKHAM
Techniques Photography: KARL ADAMSON
Food Techniques Stylist: ANGELA KINGSBURY
Recipe Testing: EMMA-LEE GOW

ISBN 0 09 180707 7

Typeset in Gill Sans by Textype Typesetters, Cambridge
Colour Separations by Magnacraft, London
Printed and bound in Italy by New Interlitho Italia S.p.a., Milan

CONTENTS

COOKERY NOTES

- Both metric and imperial measures are given for the recipes. Follow either metric or imperial throughout as they are not interchangeable.
- All spoon measures are level unless otherwise stated. Sets of measuring spoons are available in metric and imperial for accurate measurements of small quantities.
- Ovens should be preheated to the specified temperature. Grills should also be preheated. The cooking times given in the recipes assume that this has been done.
- Where a stage is specified in brackets under freezing, the dish should be frozen at the end of that stage.
- Size 2 eggs should be used except where otherwise specified. Free-range eggs are recommended.
- Use freshly ground black pepper and sea salt unless otherwise specified.
- Use fresh rather than dried herbs unless dried herbs are suggested in the recipe.
- Stocks should be freshly made if possible. Alternatively buy ready-made stocks or use good quality stock cubes.

INTRODUCTION

To many of us Thailand conjures up a vision of the exotic, a country steeped in mystery and culture. The Thai people are a passionate race and this is expressed by many things: their religion, their architecture and of course their food. They have a saying "*gan gin gan yuu*" which means: as you eat, so you are; an expression that parallels that of Brillat-Savarin "You are what you eat".

However the Thai's total commitment to food goes further than eating. It is also evident in their attitude to the ingredients they use, the preparation and presentation of their food. There is a balance of flavours, so delicate yet so evocative that their passion for food is always apparent.

The ingredients that spring to mind when we think of Thai food are chillies, ginger, fish sauce, lemon grass, limes and sugar; the flavours that these ingredients represent are hot/sweet/sour and salty. It is a paradox that Thai cooking manages to combine all these elements while still maintaining a perfect harmony.

Agriculture is the largest industry in Thailand and rice is the main staple food produced. It is therefore hardly surprising that it plays an important role in Thai cooking. In fact rice is the most important dish in every Thai meal and other dishes – such as soups, curries and stir-fries – are served as accompaniments. This provides quite a contrast to Western cooking where generally rice is served as the accompaniment. Thai rice, or Thai fragrant rice as it is often called here, can be bought in some supermarkets or from Oriental food stores. It is a very high quality long-grain rice with a soft, light, fluffy texture if correctly cooked.

Chillies were introduced into Thailand by the Portuguese in the sixteenth century and were immediately adopted as an important flavouring. Many traditional Thai dishes would be far too hot for the Western palate so the quantity of chillies in most of these recipes has been reduced to enable you to enjoy all the other flavours present. You can of course adjust the chilli quantities as desired.

Another Thai tradition that is alien to Western meals is that of serving all the food together rather than in courses. A whole selection of different dishes are set at the table at one go, all chosen to complement each other to achieve a perfect balance of flavours and textures. For example, a hot and sour soup may be served with a sweet/sour coconut curry, a tangy stir-fried beef noodle dish and, of course, plenty of delicious Thai rice.

Thai people love to entertain and it is not unusual to find large groups sitting down to a table groaning with exciting dishes. For convenience, most of the recipes in this book serve 4, although the ingredients can easily be adapted to serve larger (or smaller) numbers.

There is a tendency to assume that cooking Thai food means hours of lengthy preparation and cooking. It is true that there is often a long list of ingredients in a recipe, but much of the work is simple and surprisingly quick. Most of the preparation can be done well ahead of time and the cooking times for the majority of dishes are very short. I have been careful to include some recipes which are quick to prepare too.

The recipes are divided into chapters as follows: Starters and Snacks; Soups; Salads; Main Course Dishes; Rice, Noodles and Vegetables; and Desserts. Although this is not entirely authentic in Thai cooking it makes meal planning more practical. I prefer to serve a choice of two starters and follow this with a salad dish; a main-course dish and either a vegetable, rice or noodle dish, depending on my mood. I then finish off the meal with one of the desserts.

A Thai meal is a flexible event and the only hard and fast rule is that it is to be enjoyed in a happy and relaxed manner. Perhaps to truly appreciate all these things a trip to Thailand is necessary, but I hope that the recipes in this book will at least give you an insight into a cuisine that is exciting, exotic and totally addictive!

GUIDE TO INGREDIENTS

BAMBOO SHOOTS

The tender shoots of the bamboo plant have an acceptable crunchy texture. They are available sliced and halved in cans.

BASIL

Several different types of basil are used in Thailand but ordinary basil works well. Sweet basil can be found in some Oriental stores and as the name implies this variety has a particularly sweet flavour.

BEAN SPROUTS

These are the crisp shoots of the mung bean and are widely available from supermarkets and healthfood stores. They add a crisp texture to salads and stir-fries.

BLACK BEAN SAUCE

This thick, dark brown, salty sauce is made from fermented soya beans. It is used to add flavour to sauces and stir-fries. Available from larger supermarkets, once opened black bean sauce should be stored, tightly closed, in the refrigerator for no longer than 1 month.

CHILLIES

Fresh green and red chillies are used extensively in Thai cooking. Red chillies are simply ripe green chillies; their flavour usually differs although the intensity is often the same. In general, the smaller chillies tend to be hotter. Remove seeds for a milder flavour.

Dried chillies can be bought whole or crushed, as chilli flakes. Both include the seeds which are very fiery and are generally best removed.

CHILLI SAUCE

Hot chilli sauce, sometimes called *sambal olek*, is used in many Thai dishes. It is widely available, but ordinary chilli sauce can be used if preferred.

COCONUT

Coconut milk is used extensively in Thai dishes and is particularly good for thickening soups and curries. It is available in cans from most supermarkets and ethnic stores.

Creamed coconut is available in blocks and only a small amount is needed to both flavour and thicken a sauce. Available from most supermarkets.

Dried grated coconut flakes are available from most good healthfood stores. Unsweetened desiccated coconut can be substituted.

CORIANDER

Fresh coriander leaves are used to flavour many Thai dishes.

Coriander roots are also used to flavour spice pastes. Some good greengrocers and ethnic stores sell large bunches of coriander with the roots still attached; scrub well before use. Coriander stalks can be used instead.

CURRY PASTE

Red curry paste and green curry paste form the basis of many Thai curries. Recipes are given for both of these overleaf, but they are also available commercially from some supermarkets, Oriental stores and directly by mail order (see page 80). Once opened, reseal and store in the refrigerator for up to 1 month.

Indian curry pastes are also used in a few of the recipes. These are readily available – in mild, medium and hot strengths.

FISH SAUCE

This is called *nam pla* in Thailand and is used rather like soy sauce. It is readily available from Oriental food stores and larger supermarkets but light soy sauce can be substituted if necessary.

GALANGAL

This is a member of the ginger family and is similar in appearance, but with a slightly transparent pink-tinged skin and dark rings. It has a milder, but more aromatic flavour than root ginger and is now available from some larger supermarkets as well as Oriental food stores. (Illustrated on page 5.)

KAFFIR LIME LEAVES

The leaves of the kaffir lime tree have a very aromatic lime flavour and are frequently included in Thai dishes. There is no real substitute, although freshly grated lime rind may be used as a last resort. The fresh leaves are available from Oriental food stores and can be frozen for future use.

LEMON GRASS

A tall, hard grass, pale green in colour, available from some supermarkets and Oriental stores. The very tough outer leaves should be discarded and the rest roughly chopped to use as a flavouring. It can also be chopped and then ground with other spices to form a paste. Lemon grass can be frozen whole. (Illustrated on page 5.)

MUSHROOMS, DRIED

Dried black mushrooms are the commonest variety used in Thai cooking. They are only available from Oriental stores or by mail order, and need to be soaked in boiling water for 20-30 minutes before use.

Dried shiitake are also used in these recipes. Soak as above.

NOODLES

Dried egg thread noodles, thin and medium, are available from most supermarkets and delicatessens.

Dried rice noodles are used extensively in Thai cooking. These are flatter than the egg noodles similar to tagliatelle, but are whiter and more transparent in appearance. (Illustrated on page 5.) Dried rice vermicelli are a finer version.

For all noodles, follow the cooking instructions on the packet.

OYSTER SAUCE

This is thick Chinese sauce which is sweet and salty at the same time. It is used to flavour many dishes and is widely available from supermarkets.

PAK CHOI

A Chinese leaf vegetable often used in stir-fry dishes, available from some supermarkets and Oriental shops. Chinese cabbage is a good alternative. (Illustrated on page 5.)

PEANUTS

These nuts are particularly synonymous with Thai cooking and are added to sauces as well as used as a condiment for curries and salads. Buy raw unsalted nuts with or without their reddish skins. To toast peanuts or other whole nuts, place on a baking sheet and roast in a preheated oven at 200°C (400°F) Mark 6 for 8-10 minutes until golden.

RICE

Rice is served at every Thai meal. Thai fragrant rice, available from most supermarkets, is quite delicious if correctly cooked. To cook perfect Thai rice, wash 225 g (8 oz) Thai fragrant rice in cold water for several minutes until the water runs clear. Put the rice in a heavy-based saucepan and add 300 ml (½ pint) cold water. Cover and bring quickly to the boil. As soon as the water boils, remove the lid and stir over a medium heat until all the water has evaporated. Replace the lid (making sure it fits tightly) and set over a low heat for 20 minutes allowing the rice to steam. The resulting rice should be soft, light and fluffy.

RICE FLOUR

Used in many Thai dishes, this is similar in texture and taste to cornflour. It can be bought at most Oriental stores as well as good healthfood stores.

RICE VINEGAR

This is also called mirin and, as the name suggests, is made from rice. It is available from good healthfood shops, some delicatessens and Oriental stores. Use sherry or white wine vinegar as an alternative.

SHRIMP, DRIED; SHRIMP PASTE

Packets of dried shrimp are available from ethnic stores and are used in Thai pastes. There is no real substitute for dried shrimp, but they are also available by mail order (see page 80).

Shrimp paste, or *nam prik* as it is called in Thailand, is made from dried shrimps and used to flavour many pastes and sauces. It is available commercially from Oriental stores and by mail order.

SOY SAUCE

Although soy sauce is rarely used in Thailand as fish sauce predominates, both dark and light soy sauces are used in these recipes, as well as a thick sweet soy sauce which is available commercially as *kecap manis*. To make this at home combine 120 ml (4 fl oz) dark soy sauce with 45 ml (3 tbsp) molasses and 22 ml (1½ tbsp) dark brown sugar in a saucepan. Heat gently, stirring until the sugar is dissolved.

SZECHUAN PEPPERCORNS

These are reddish-brown peppercorns and are very aromatic. They are available from most supermarkets.

TAMARIND PASTE

This is a bean paste made from the tamarind plant, sold in a block form. To make tamarind paste, break 25 g

(1 oz) off the block and blend in 45 ml (3 tbsp) hot water. Press and use as required. Lemon juice can be used instead.

TOFU

Firm tofu, available in block form, is used in many Thai vegetable dishes. It is made from fermented and pressed soya beans. Although rather bland in flavour it readily absorbs the flavours of foods that it is cooked with. Drain off the liquid from the packet and cut the tofu into cubes.

WATERCHESTNUTS

These are available whole in cans from most supermarkets. Drain well and pat dry before using.

WONTON WRAPPERS

Small thin squares of dough, sold fresh or frozen in most Oriental food stores; also available by mail order (see page 80). Alternatively you can make your own (see page 28).

YARD LONG BEANS

Available from ethnic stores, these are long thin beans similar to French beans but 3-4 times longer. (Illustrated on page 5.) Substitute French beans if necessary.

RED CURRY PASTE

2 long thin fresh red chillies
8 dried red chillies
4 kaffir lime leaves
2.5 cm (1 inch) piece galangal
4 shallots
4 garlic cloves
2 lemon grass stalks
5 ml (1 tsp) ground black pepper
5 ml (1 tsp) turmeric
30 ml (2 tbsp) sunflower oil

1. Halve and deseed the fresh and dried chillies, wearing rubber gloves to prevent skin irritation, then roughly chop the chillies and lime leaves.

2. Peel and chop the galangal, shallots and garlic.

3. Peel and finely chop the lemon grass.

4. Purée the prepared ingredients in a spice grinder or blender with the black pepper, turmeric and sunflower oil to form a smooth paste. Store in a screw-topped jar for up to 1 month.

GREEN CURRY PASTE

4 long thin green chillies
2-4 small green chillies
4 garlic cloves
2.5 cm (1 inch) piece fresh root ginger
6 spring onions, trimmed
4 coriander roots, scrubbed
1 lemon grass stalk
4 kaffir lime leaves
15 ml (1 tbsp) chopped fresh coriander

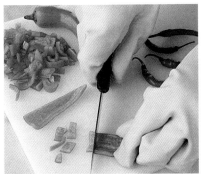

1. Wearing rubber gloves to prevent skin irritation, halve the large and small chillies, deseed if preferred, then roughly chop.

2. Peel and chop the chillies, garlic and ginger.

3. Chop the spring onions and coriander roots.

4. Peel and finely chop the lemon grass. Shred the lime leaves.

5. Place all the ingredients in a spice grinder or mortar. Grind or pound to form a smooth paste, adding a little water if necessary. Store in a screw-topped jar for up to 1 month.

GOLDEN PRAWN CUPS

Traditionally little golden cups of batter are shaped and deep-fried using a special metal ladle, then filled with various spicy mixtures. This technique is quite difficult to perfect so here I have used filo pastry as a simple and satisfactory alternative.

SERVES 4

4 sheets filo pastry, thawed
 if frozen
sunflower oil
TOMATO SAUCE
4 ripe tomatoes
2 shallots, peeled
I cm (½ inch) piece fresh
 root ginger, peeled
15 ml (I tbsp) sweet soy
 sauce
15 ml (I tbsp) lemon juice
15 ml (I tbsp) chopped
 fresh coriander
salt and pepper
PRAWN FILLING
225 g (8 oz) small raw tiger
 prawns
I bunch spring onions,
 trimmed
2 garlic cloves, peeled
I small red chilli, seeded
125 g (4 oz) button
 mushrooms
50 g (2 oz) mangetout
15 ml (I tbsp) chopped
 fresh coriander
10 ml (2 tsp) grated lemon
 rind
pinch of salt
pinch of sugar
15 ml (I tbsp) light soy sauce
15 g (½ oz) cashew nuts,
 toasted
TO GARNISH
spring onion shreds

PREPARATION TIME 30 minutes
COOKING TIME 12-15 minutes
FREEZING Suitable: Stage 3. Freeze sauce
and cups separately. Open freeze filo cups.

265 CALS PER SERVING

I. Preheat the oven to 200°C (400°F) Mark 6. Cut each sheet of pastry into four 10 cm (4 inch) squares. Brush one square of pastry with a little oil and lightly press over an upturned ramekin dish. Brush a further three squares with oil and arrange on top to make a star-shaped case (see technique).

2. Repeat with remaining pastry to make 4 cases. Transfer to a baking sheet and bake for 12-15 minutes until golden. Remove from the oven and leave to cool. Carefully ease the cases away from the ramekins and place the right way up. Set aside.

3. Meanwhile, make the sauce. Immerse the tomatoes in boiling water for 30 seconds, then drain, refresh under cold water and peel away the skins. Quarter, deseed and dice the flesh. Finely chop the shallots and grate the ginger. Heat 15 ml (I tbsp) sunflower oil in a small pan, add the shallots and ginger and fry gently for 3 minutes until softened. Add the tomatoes, stir-fry for 3 minutes, then add the soy sauce, lemon juice and coriander. Heat through for I minute, then remove from the heat. Season with salt and pepper to taste.

4. Make the prawn filling. Cut the heads off the prawns and peel away the shells. Make a shallow slit down the back of each prawn and remove the dark intestinal vein. Rinse thoroughly and pat dry. Finely slice the spring onions, garlic and chilli. Heat 15 ml (I tbsp) sunflower oil in a wok or frying pan, add the onions, garlic and chilli and fry for 3 minutes.

5. Slice the mushrooms. Add a little extra oil to the pan and add the mushrooms. Stir-fry for 30 seconds, then add the prawns and mangetout and continue to stir-fry for a further 2-3 minutes, until the prawns are pink. Add the remaining ingredients, cover the pan and heat gently for 2 minutes.

6. Spoon the filling into the pastry cups, garnish with spring onions shreds and serve at once, with the tomato sauce.

TECHNIQUE

Layer 4 squares of filo pastry over each upturned ramekin, positioning each at a slightly different angle to form a case.

PRAWN ROLLS

Raw prawns are rolled in thin strips of filo pastry and deep-fried until crisp and golden. These traditional Thai snacks are fun to make and eat with their tails protruding cheekily from the pastry. They are served with a sweet and sour dipping sauce.

SERVES 4

2 spring onions, trimmed

1 garlic clove, peeled

1.25 ml (¼ tsp) salt

5 ml (1 tsp) grated fresh
   root ginger

5 ml (1 tsp) red curry paste
   (see page 6 or 8)

15 ml (1 tbsp) chopped fresh
   coriander

5 ml (1 tsp) tamarind paste
   (see page 8)

1.25 ml (¼ tsp) sugar

16 large raw tiger prawns

4-8 sheets filo pastry

1 egg white, beaten

vegetable oil, for deep-frying

DIPPING SAUCE

2 small red chillies

50 g (2 oz) caster sugar

50 ml (2 fl oz) rice vinegar

2.5 ml (½ tsp) salt

PREPARATION TIME
40 minutes
COOKING TIME
About 10 minutes
FREEZING
Not suitable

320 CALS PER SERVING

1. Start by making the dipping sauce. Finely chop the chillies, discarding the seeds if preferred, then place in a small pan with the sugar, vinegar, salt and 30 ml (2 tbsp) water. Bring slowly to the boil, stirring until the sugar is dissolved, then remove from the heat and set aside to cool.

2. To make the prawn rolls, roughly chop the spring onions and garlic. Grind to a smooth paste with the salt, ginger, red curry paste and coriander, using a spice grinder or pestle and mortar. Stir in the tamarind paste and sugar.

3. Cut the heads off the prawns, then peel away the shells. Make a slit down the back of each prawn and remove the dark intestinal vein. Rinse well and pat dry. Cut the filo pastry into 16 strips, each 7.5 cm (3 inches) wide and 15 cm (6 inches) long. Keep covered with a lightly dampened tea-towel.

4. Working with one strip of pastry at a time, brush lightly with a little egg white. Spread 5 ml (1 tsp) of the spice mixture at one end of the pastry strip, top with a prawn and roll the pastry up to enclose all but the tail. Repeat to make 16 rolls.

5. Heat a 10 cm (4 inch) depth of oil in a deep, heavy-based saucepan to 180°C (350°F) as registered on a thermometer or until a cube of bread dropped into the oil browns in 30 seconds. Fry the prawn

rolls in the hot oil in batches for 2-3 minutes until crisp and golden. Drain on kitchen paper and serve hot with the sweet and sour dipping sauce.

VARIATION

Instead of wrapping the prawns in filo, coat them in a light batter. Blend 50 g (2 oz) rice flour with 1 (size 1) egg and 90 ml (3 fl oz) iced water until smooth. Dip the prepared prawns in a little plain flour, then into the batter. Fry in hot oil for 1-2 minutes until golden and crisp.

TECHNIQUE

Roll each spiced prawn in a strip of filo pastry to enclose all but the tail.

GRILLED KING PRAWNS WITH CHILLI SOY SAUCE

This is a dish that definitely requires a finger bowl! It's a messy business, but what could be better than dipping succulent grilled prawns into a rich, tangy soy dip? If preferred the prawns can be threaded onto bamboo skewers and grilled or barbecued.

SERVES 4

12 large raw tiger prawns
MARINADE
1 garlic clove, peeled
1 red chilli, seeded
15 ml (1 tbsp) sesame oil
30 ml (2 tbsp) dark soy
   sauce
grated rind and juice of 2
   limes
15-30 ml (1-2 tbsp) soft
   brown sugar
CHILLI SOY SAUCE
5 ml (1 tsp) crushed chilli
   flakes
15 ml (1 tbsp) lime juice
30 ml (2 tbsp) dark soy
   sauce
15 ml (1 tbsp) Thai fish
   sauce
30 ml (2 tbsp) soft brown
   sugar
TO SERVE
chopped fresh coriander
lime wedges

PREPARATION TIME
20 minutes, plus marinating
COOKING TIME
6-8 minutes
FREEZING
Not suitable

115 CALS PER SERVING

1. Wash and dry the prawns and place in a shallow non-reactive dish. To make the marinade, finely chop the garlic and chilli and mix with the remaining ingredients. Pour over the prawns and stir well to coat. Cover the dish and leave to marinate in a cool place for at least 4 hours, preferably overnight.

2. For the chilli soy sauce, place all the ingredients in a small pan with 30 ml (2 tbsp) cold water and bring to the boil, stirring until the sugar is dissolved. Remove the pan from the heat and leave to cool.

3. Just before serving, preheat the grill. Transfer the prawns to the grill pan and grill as close to the heat as possible for 6-8 minutes, turning and basting frequently with the marinade juices, until the prawns are pink and lightly charred.

4. Transfer the prawns to a warmed serving platter and scatter over some chopped fresh coriander. Serve with lime wedges and the chilli sauce for dipping. Don't forget the finger bowls!

VARIATION

Pre-soak 4 bamboo skewers in water for 30 minutes, drain and thread 3 marinated prawns onto each skewer. Grill as close to the heat as possible for 2-3 minutes on each side until charred and cooked through. Serve with the chilli soy sauce.

TECHNIQUE

Turn the prawns and baste frequently with the marinade during grilling to keep them moist.

BATTERED MUSSELS WITH CARAMELISED CHILLI PASTE

Lightly steamed mussels are coated in a coconut and chive flavoured batter then deep-fried to perfection. Pickled cabbage and a thick, tangy chilli sauce that is sweet, like a jam, accompany these exotic morsels. Serve them as part of a selection of starter dishes.

SERVES 4

48 large fresh mussels in shells
50 g (2 oz) plain flour
15 g (½ oz) rice flour or
  cornflour
2.5 ml (½ tsp) salt
15 g (½ oz) desiccated
  coconut
15 ml (1 tbsp) chopped fresh
  chives
½ egg (or 1 size 5), beaten
15 ml (1 tbsp) rice wine or
  dry sherry
vegetable oil, for deep frying
PICKLED CABBAGE
125 g (4 oz) white cabbage
120 ml (4 fl oz) white wine
  vinegar
2 shallots, peeled
1 garlic clove, peeled
15 ml (1 tbsp) sesame oil
CHILLI PASTE
2 shallots, peeled
1 garlic clove, peeled
15 ml (1 tbsp) sunflower oil
15 ml (1 tbsp) hot chilli sauce
50 g (2 oz) dark muscovado
  sugar
30 ml (2 tbsp) lemon juice
5 ml (1 tsp) salt
30 ml (2 tbsp) light soy sauce
TO GARNISH
lemon wedges and chives

PREPARATION TIME 25 minutes
COOKING TIME 25-30 minutes
FREEZING Not suitable

465 CALS PER SERVING

1. First prepare the pickled cabbage. Shred the cabbage. Bring the vinegar to the boil in a small pan, then add the cabbage and simmer for 1 minute. Remove from the heat. Finely chop the shallots and garlic. Heat the oil in a pan, add the shallots and garlic and fry for 2-3 minutes until softened. Stir in the cabbage and vinegar and simmer gently for 5 minutes. Set aside to cool.

2. Make the chilli paste. Finely chop the shallots and garlic and fry in the oil for 3 minutes until softened. Add the remaining ingredients, bring to the boil and simmer fast for 3-4 minutes until the sauce is reduced and syrupy. Remove from the heat and leave to cool.

3. Scrub the mussels thoroughly under cold running water and remove their beards. Discard damaged ones and any that remain open when sharply tapped. Steam the mussels in a tightly covered large pan with just the water clinging to the shells for 3-4 minutes until opened. Discard any that remain closed. Plunge the mussels into cold water to cool, then remove them from their shells.

4. To make the batter, sift the flours and salt into a bowl, stir in the coconut and chives, then gradually beat in the egg, wine and 100 ml (3½ fl oz) water to form a batter.

5. Heat a 10 cm (4 inch) depth of vegetable oil in a deep, heavy-based saucepan to a temperature of 180°C (350°F) as registered on a thermometer or until a cube of bread dropped into the oil browns in 30 seconds. Deep-fry the mussels in batches. Dip into the batter, then carefully tip into the oil and fry for 30 seconds to 1 minute until crisp and golden. Drain on kitchen paper and serve hot, garnished with lemon wedges and chives and accompanied by the pickled cabbage and chilli paste.

TECHNIQUE

Deep-fry the battered mussels in the hot oil until crisp, then remove with a slotted spoon and drain on kitchen paper.

GLAZED CHICKEN WINGS

Although this is not a truly authentic Thai recipe, it uses Thai spices and flavourings to make a rich glaze for the chicken wings – creating a delicious, more-ish starter similar to barbecued chicken wings. It is simple and quick to prepare, but the longer the wings are left to marinate the more flavour they absorb.

SERVES 4

12 small chicken wings
4 garlic cloves, peeled
5-10 ml (1-2 tsp) hot chilli
    sauce
45 ml (3 tbsp) sweet soy
    sauce
15 ml (1 tbsp) preserved stem
    ginger syrup or clear honey
15 ml (1 tbsp) lemon juice
5 ml (1 tsp) ground
    coriander
2.5 ml (½ tsp) ground
    cinnamon
TO GARNISH
spring onion shreds
lime and/or lemon wedges

PREPARATION TIME
10 minutes, plus marinating
COOKING TIME
About 1 hour
FREEZING
Not suitable

175 CALS PER SERVING

1. Wash and dry the chicken wings and pull out any small feathers that still remain attached. Tuck the tip of each wing under the thickest part of the wing, forming a triangular shape. Transfer to a large shallow, non-reactive dish.

2. Crush the garlic and place in a bowl. Add all the remaining ingredients, mix well, then pour over the chicken wings. Toss to coat the wings thoroughly. Cover and leave to marinate in a cool place for at least 4 hours, preferably overnight.

3. Preheat the oven to 220°C (425°F) Mark 7. Transfer the chicken wings and marinade juices to a roasting tin just large enough to hold them in a single layer. Bake at the top of the oven for 50-60 minutes, basting and turning frequently until the wings are glazed and tender. The flesh should almost fall from the bone. Serve hot, garnished with spring onion shreds and lime and/or lemon wedges. Remember to provide finger bowls.

VARIATION

Use the sauce as a glaze for spare ribs rather than chicken wings. Place 675 g (1½ lb) pork ribs in a pan, cover with cold water and add 30 ml (2 tbsp) distilled malt vinegar. Bring to the boil and simmer for 20 minutes, then drain and cool. Toss with the marinade and continue as above.

TECHNIQUE

Tuck the tip of each chicken wing under the thickest part of the wing, to form a triangle.

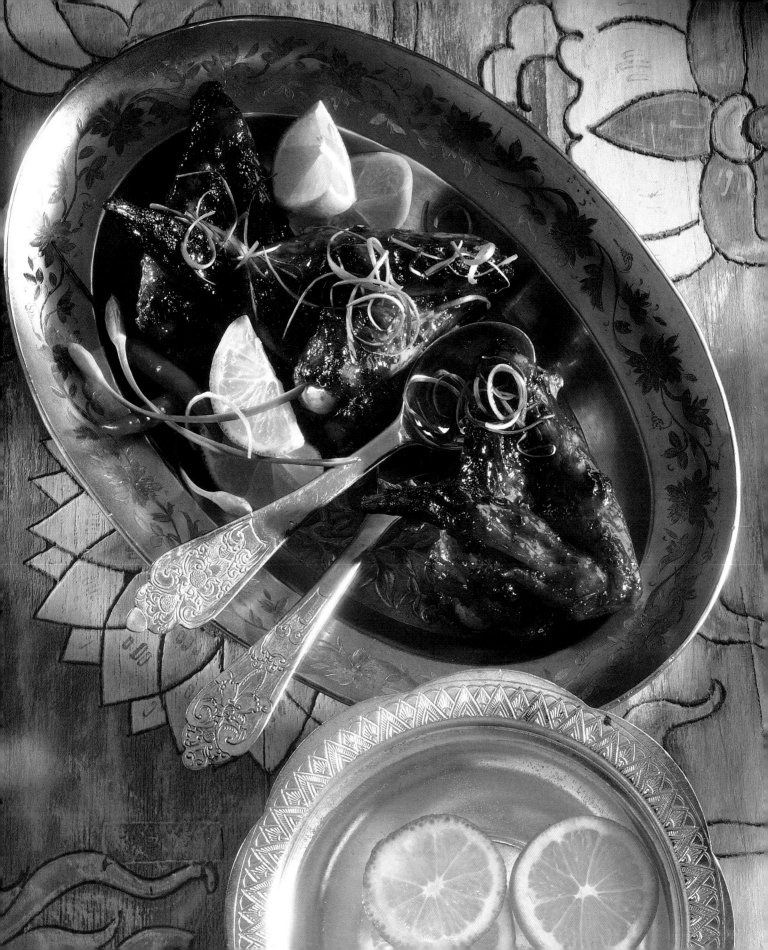

BEEF SATAY

This Thai snack is very simple to make and quite delicious to eat. Strips of beef are marinated for several hours, threaded onto bamboo skewers and grilled until charred and tender. They are served with a peanut dipping sauce and cubes of chilled cooked rice which provide a cool, refreshing balance to the spicy beef.

SERVES 4

350 g (12 oz) fillet steak
2 garlic cloves, peeled
2.5 cm (1 inch) piece fresh
　root ginger, peeled
30 ml (2 tbsp) dark soy sauce
30 ml (2 tbsp) sweet sherry
15 ml (1 tbsp) rice or wine
　vinegar
10 ml (2 tsp) sesame oil
2.5 ml ($\frac{1}{2}$ tsp) chilli powder
RICE CUBES
50 g (2 oz) Thai fragrant rice
salt
PEANUT SAUCE
60 ml (4 tbsp) chopped
　peanuts
1.25 ml ($\frac{1}{4}$ tsp) crushed chilli
　flakes
1 garlic clove, crushed
15 ml (1 tbsp) dark soy sauce
15 ml (1 tbsp) lime juice
5 ml (1 tsp) thin honey
$\frac{1}{2}$ x 200 g (7 oz) packet
　creamed coconut

PREPARATION TIME
30 minutes, plus freezing and
marinating
COOKING TIME
20 minutes
FREEZING
Not suitable

110 CALS PER SERVING

1. Place the beef in the freezer for 30 minutes until firm (to make it easier to slice).

2. Using a sharp knife, slice the beef across the grain into thin strips. Place in a shallow non-reactive dish. Crush the garlic and grate the ginger; place in a bowl with the soy sauce, sherry, vinegar, sesame oil and chilli powder. Pour over the beef, stir well, cover and leave to marinate in a cool place for 2-4 hours.

3. Cook the rice in boiling salted water for 15 minutes until very soft. Drain and refresh under cold water. Drain thoroughly. Press the rice into a small oiled dish and smooth the surface. Chill in the refrigerator until required.

4. Preheat the grill. Remove the beef from the marinade and thread onto bamboo skewers in a zig-zag fashion. Place the beef skewers on the grill rack and grill as close to the heat as possible for 4-5 minutes until tender, turning halfway through cooking.

5. Meanwhile make the peanut sauce. Put the peanuts, chilli flakes, garlic, soy sauce, lime juice and honey in a small pan and heat gently. Add the creamed coconut and cook, stirring, until smooth. Remove from the heat. Unmould the rice and cut into cubes. Serve the beef satay with the peanut dipping sauce and rice cubes.

VARIATION

For a vegetarian alternative, choose a selection of root vegetables and cut into small, equal-sized cubes. Marinate as above, thread the vegetables alternately onto the skewers and grill until golden and tender. Serve with the peanut sauce and rice cubes.

TECHNIQUE

Thread the marinated beef strips onto the skewers in a zig-zag fashion.

SWEET POTATO CAKES WITH BAKED GARLIC

Sweet potatoes are often eaten in Thailand, in the way we serve chips. Here they form the basis of tasty potato cakes flavoured with coriander and coconut. These are served with baked garlic and a tangy prawn paste, called *nam prik*. This prawn paste is a staple condiment in Thailand and can be served as a sauce or stirred into other dishes. You can make it yourself, or buy it ready-made from Oriental food suppliers.

SERVES 4

BAKED GARLIC
2 heads of garlic, about 125 g
  (4 oz) total weight
15 ml (1 tbsp) dark soy sauce
15 ml (1 tbsp) lemon juice
pinch of salt
pinch of sugar
PRAWN PASTE
2 garlic cloves, peeled
2-3 small green chillies,
  seeded
1.25 ml (¼ tsp) sea salt
30 ml (2 tbsp) dried shrimp
15 ml (1 tbsp) Thai fish sauce
15 ml (1 tbsp) dark
  muscovado sugar
30 ml (2 tbsp) lemon juice
POTATO CAKES
450 g (1 lb) sweet potatoes
225 g (8 oz) potato
15 g (½ oz) fresh coriander
  roots
30 ml (2 tbsp) chopped fresh
  coriander leaves
50 g (2 oz) desiccated
  coconut, toasted
15 g (½ oz) plain flour
5 ml (1 tsp) sesame oil
flour, for dusting
50 g (2 oz) sesame seeds
oil for shallow-frying

PREPARATION TIME 45 minutes
COOKING TIME 50 minutes
FREEZING Suitable: Potato cakes only
(stage 4)

470 CALS PER SERVING

1. Preheat the oven to 200°C (400°F) Mark 6. Cut a small slice from the top of each garlic head and sit on a double layer of foil. Combine the soy sauce, lemon juice, salt and sugar in a bowl, then pour over the garlic. Seal the foil and bake for 30 minutes. Set aside until required.

2. Meanwhile, make the prawn paste. Roughly chop the garlic and chillies and grind to a smooth paste with the salt and dried shrimp, using a spice grinder or a pestle and mortar. Transfer to a dish and stir in the remaining ingredients. Set aside.

3. For the potato cakes, peel and cube all the potatoes and place in a saucepan. Scrub and chop the coriander roots and add to the pan. Add plenty of cold water to cover, bring to the boil and cook for 12-15 minutes until tender. Drain, return to the heat for a few seconds to dry out the potato, then mash with a potato masher. Allow to cool slightly.

4. Stir in the chopped coriander, coconut, flour and sesame oil. Season with salt and pepper to taste. With lightly floured hands, form the mixture into 12 small patties.

5. Dip the potato cakes in the sesame seeds to coat. Heat a shallow layer of oil in a heavy-based, non-stick frying pan. Fry the potato cakes in batches for 2-3 minutes each side until golden and heated through. Drain on kitchen paper.

6. Serve the potato cakes hot with the caramelised garlic cloves and a spoonful of prawn paste.

VARIATION

Serve with Thai tomato sauce (see page 10) rather than prawn paste.

TECHNIQUE

Using lightly floured hands, shape the mixture into 12 flat round cakes.

SPRING ROLLS WITH CUCUMBER RELISH

This is another classic Thai snack which also makes a delicious starter dish. Traditionally wonton skins or rice wrappers are used for spring rolls, but I find filo pastry a convenient alternative.

SERVES 4

25 g (1 oz) rice vermicelli
   noodles
50 g (2 oz) carrot
50 g (2 oz) mangetout
15 ml (1 tbsp) sunflower oil
5 ml (1 tsp) grated fresh
   galangal or root ginger
grated rind and juice of 1 lime
25 g (1 oz) spinach leaves
30 ml (2 tbsp) Thai fish sauce
15 ml (1 tbsp) each chopped
   fresh mint and coriander
pepper, to taste
6 sheets filo pastry, thawed
   if frozen
1 egg white, lightly beaten
vegetable oil, for deep-frying
CUCUMBER RELISH
1 small red chilli, seeded
50 g (2 oz) caster sugar
60 ml (2 fl oz) rice vinegar
2.5 ml (½ tsp) salt
1 small tomato
50 g (2 oz) cucumber

PREPARATION TIME
30 minutes
COOKING TIME
8-10 minutes
FREEZING Suitable: Uncooked
rolls only. Deep-fry from frozen
for 5 minutes (or thaw first).

270 CALS PER SERVING

1. Soak the vermicelli noodles according to the packet instructions; drain, refresh under cold water and shake dry. Using scissors, snip the noodles into short lengths, about 2.5 cm (1 inch) long.

2. Cut the carrot and mangetout into matchsticks. Heat the oil in a wok or large frying pan and stir-fry the galangal or ginger, lime rind, carrot and mangetout for 3 minutes. Add the remaining ingredients, together with the noodles, and stir-fry for 1 minute. Remove the pan from the heat and set aside to cool.

3. Meanwhile make the relish. Place the chilli, sugar, vinegar, salt and 30 ml (2 tbsp) water in a small pan. Stir slowly until the sugar is dissolved and the mixture boils. Remove from the heat. Peel, deseed and dice the tomato; halve, deseed and slice the cucumber. Stir the tomato and cucumber into the relish and set aside.

4. Cut the filo pastry into 18 cm (7 inch) squares, then halve each square diagonally to make 2 triangles. Take one triangle, brush with a little egg white and place a spoonful of the noodle mixture at the point opposite the longest side. Roll the pastry over the filling, folding the sides in as you go, to form a small spring roll. Press the seam together well and repeat to make 12 rolls.

5. Heat a 10 cm (4 inch) depth of oil in a deep saucepan until it registers 180°C (350°) on a thermometer or until a cube of bread dropped into the oil browns in 30 seconds. Deep-fry the rolls, in batches, for 2-3 minutes until crisp and golden. Drain on kitchen paper and serve hot with the cucumber relish.

NOTE: When using filo pastry always work with one sheet at a time. Keep the rest covered with a lightly dampened tea-towel to stop it from drying out.

TECHNIQUE

Place a spoonful of noodle mixture at the point opposite the longest side. Roll up from this point, folding in the sides as you do so.

VEGETABLE, NOODLE AND TOFU BROTH

This soup is a particular favourite of mine as the flavours are light, refreshing and quite delicate. Its success depends on the quality of the stock, which is used to poach a selection of vegetables and the tofu. The following recipe gives an authentic Thai stock, which is used as the basis for other recipes in this chapter too.

SERVES 4

STOCK
1.2 litres (2 pints) water
1 onion, peeled
2 carrots
2 celery sticks
2 garlic cloves, peeled
2 lemon grass stalks
15 g (½ oz) fresh root
   ginger
4 kaffir lime leaves
4 coriander roots, scrubbed
5 ml (1 tsp) white
   peppercorns
5 ml (1 tsp) salt
BROTH
25 g (1 oz) dried black or
   shiitake mushrooms
120 ml (4 fl oz) boiling water
1 large carrot
50 g (2 oz) cauliflower
   florets
50 g (2 oz) baby sweetcorn
125 g (4 oz) plain tofu
30 ml (2 tbsp) dark soy sauce
15 ml (1 tbsp) lemon or lime
   juice
50 g (2 oz) dried egg thread
   noodles
TO SERVE
mint leaves
chilli oil

PREPARATION TIME 20 minutes
COOKING TIME 1¼ hours, including stock
FREEZING Suitable: Stock only

135 CALS PER SERVING

1. Start by making the stock. Place the water in a large saucepan. Roughly chop the onion, carrots, celery, garlic, lemon grass and ginger and add to the pan with the remaining ingredients. Bring to the boil, cover and simmer over a gentle heat for 1 hour.

2. Put the dried mushrooms in a bowl, pour over the boiling water and leave to soak for 30 minutes. Strain and reserve the liquid; chop the mushrooms.

3. Prepare the remaining vegetables. Cut the carrot into matchsticks; divide the cauliflower into small florets; halve the sweetcorn lengthways; set aside. Cube the tofu.

4. Strain the stock into a clean pan and stir in the soy sauce, lemon or lime juice and reserved mushroom liquid. Return to the boil and stir in the prepared vegetables, tofu and soaked mushrooms. Simmer for 5 minutes.

5. Plunge in the noodles and simmer for a further 5-6 minutes until the noodles and vegetables are tender. Ladle the soup into large warmed soup bowls. Serve at once, scattered with mint leaves and drizzled with a little chilli oil.

VARIATIONS

If you haven't time to prepare the stock, make up the required amount of liquid using a vegetable stock cube and add 15 ml (1 tbsp) each of lime and lemon juice and a pinch of sugar. Alternatively, use a good quality chicken stock instead.

TECHNIQUE

To prepare the vegetables, cut the carrot into matchstick strips, divide the cauliflower into small florets and halve the sweetcorn lengthways.

HOT AND SOUR SOUP WITH CRAB-STUFFED WONTONS

Although wontons are often associated with Chinese soups they are also found in traditional Thai dishes. Wonton wrappers can be bought in Oriental stores but if you are unable to find any try making them yourself (see below); they are simple and very satisfying to prepare.

SERVES 4

1.2 litres (2 pints) vegetable stock (see page 26)

4 small red chillies, bruised

15 ml (1 tbsp) Thai fish sauce

30 ml (2 tbsp) rice vinegar

15 ml (1 tbsp) chilli sauce (optional)

CRAB WONTONS

125 g (4 oz) white crab meat, fresh or frozen and thawed

50 g (2 oz) cooked peeled prawns

2 spring onions, trimmed

1 garlic clove, crushed

5 ml (1 tsp) chopped preserved stem ginger

5 ml (1 tsp) ginger syrup (from preserved ginger jar)

1.25 ml (¼ tsp) chilli powder

15 ml (1 tbsp) light soy sauce

30 ml (2 tbsp) chopped fresh coriander

16 wonton wrappers

1 small egg, beaten

TO GARNISH

chilli oil (optional)

coriander leaves

PREPARATION TIME 30 minutes
COOKING TIME 15 minutes, plus stock
FREEZING Not suitable

110 CALS PER SERVING

1. To prepare the wonton filling, drain the crab meat thoroughly (if frozen) and place in a bowl. Roughly chop the prawns and spring onions and add to the crab meat with the garlic, stem ginger, ginger syrup, chilli powder, soy sauce and coriander. Stir well until evenly combined.

2. Lightly brush a wonton wrapper with a little beaten egg and place a heaped teaspoon of crab mixture in the centre. Draw up the edges of the wrapper and press together at the top to seal. Repeat to make 16 wontons. Cover and set aside.

3. Strain the vegetable stock into a clean pan and add the chillies, fish sauce, vinegar and chilli sauce if using. Return to the boil and simmer gently for 10 minutes.

4. Bring the soup to a rolling boil, then add the wontons. Return to the boil, then lower the heat and simmer gently for 3-4 minutes until the wontons are softened and heated through.

5. Ladle into warmed soup bowls and serve at once, drizzled with a little chilli oil if wished, and garnished with coriander.

HOMEMADE WONTON WRAPPERS:
Sift 150 g (5 oz) plain flour with 2.5 ml (½ tsp) salt into a bowl. Gradually work in 1 egg and enough cold water to form a stiff dough. Knead for 5 minutes. Wrap and chill for 30 minutes. Roll out the dough in batches as thinly as possible, using a pasta machine if possible. Cut into 7.5 cm (3 inch) squares. Use immediately or freeze for future use.

TECHNIQUE

Place a heaped teaspoon of filling in the centre of each wonton wrapper and draw up the edges of the wrapper, pressing them together at the top to seal in the filling.

MUSSEL AND SQUID SOUP WITH TOMATOES AND GINGER

This fresh tasting, spicy seafood soup is quick and easy to prepare, especially if you make the stock up in advance. An unusual garnish of crispy fried basil leaves enhances the flavour as well as the appearance.

SERVES 4

1.2 litres (2 pints) vegetable stock (see page 26)
450 g (1 lb) fresh mussels in shells
450 g (1 lb) large squid
450 g (1 lb) tomatoes
2 garlic cloves, peeled
5 cm (2 inch) piece fresh root ginger, peeled
10 ml (2 tsp) hot chilli sauce
30 ml (2 tbsp) Thai fish sauce
30 ml (2 tbsp) tamarind paste (see page 8)
5 ml (1 tsp) dark muscovado sugar
15 ml (1 tbsp) chopped fresh basil
TO SERVE
60 ml (4 tbsp) sunflower oil
20 large basil leaves
lime wedges

PREPARATION TIME
30 minutes
COOKING TIME
About 45 minutes, plus stock
FREEZING
Not suitable

280 CALS PER SERVING

1. Strain the stock into a clean pan and boil rapidly until reduced to about 600 ml (1 pint).

2. Scrub the mussels thoroughly under cold running water and remove their beards. Discard ones with damaged shells and any that remain open when sharply tapped. Place in a large bowl, cover with cold water and leave to soak.

3. Rinse the squid then, holding the body in one hand, firmly pull the tentacles with the other hand to remove the soft contents of the body at the same time. Cut the tentacles just in front of the eyes, discarding the body contents. Squeeze out the plastic-like quill from the body and discard. Rub off the dark skin, then rinse the body cavity thoroughly. Cut the body into square pieces and score with a sharp knife. Halve the tentacles.

4. Roughly chop the tomatoes; finely chop the garlic and ginger. Stir into the reduced stock with the chilli sauce, fish sauce, tamarind paste and sugar. Return to the boil and simmer, uncovered, for 20 minutes.

5. Add the drained mussels, squid and basil and simmer for 5-6 minutes until the mussels open and the squid is tender. Discard any mussels that remain closed.

6. Meanwhile, heat the oil in a small pan and, when hot, add the basil leaves and fry for 1 minute until crisp and golden; drain on kitchen paper.

7. Serve the soup in large warmed bowls, garnished with the fried basil leaves and accompanied by the lime wedges.

VARIATION

For a richer, creamier soup, replace half the stock with 250 ml (8 fl oz) coconut milk adding it with the mussels and squid towards the end of cooking.

TECHNIQUE

Halve the squid tentacles. Cut the body into squares, then score.

COCONUT CHICKEN SOUP WITH FRESH PEAS

This dish is based on a Thai classic, with the unusual addition of fresh peas. The normal ingredient used is pea aubergines, but these are difficult to locate in this country and often have an unpleasantly bitter taste. On testing this recipe we found that fresh garden peas made a lovely alternative. Use frozen peas when fresh ones are out of season and add them to the pan from frozen.

SERVES 4

225 g (8 oz) skinless chicken
    breast fillet
MARINADE
1 garlic clove, crushed
15 ml (1 tbsp) dark soy sauce
15 ml (1 tbsp) Thai fish sauce
15 ml (1 tbsp) tamarind
    paste (see page 8)
5 ml (1 tsp) turmeric
SOUP
2 lemon grass stalks
4 kaffir lime leaves
4 coriander roots, scrubbed
900 ml (1½ pints) chicken
    stock
6 shallots, peeled
2 garlic cloves, peeled
2-4 small red chillies, seeded
2.5 cm (1 inch) piece galangal
30 ml (2 tbsp) sunflower oil
400 g (14 oz) can coconut
    milk
10 ml (2 tsp) soft brown
    sugar
125 g (4 oz) shelled fresh or
    frozen peas
TO SERVE
30 ml (2 tbsp) torn
    coriander leaves
sesame oil

PREPARATION TIME
30 minutes, plus marinating
COOKING TIME
1 hour
FREEZING
Not suitable

435 CALS PER SERVING

1. Wash and dry the chicken breast and cut across the grain into thin slices; place in a shallow non-reactive dish. Combine the ingredients for the marinade. Add to the chicken, toss well, cover and leave to marinate for at least 4 hours.

2. For the soup, roughly chop the lemon grass and lime leaves and place in a mortar with the coriander roots; pound together until well bruised. (Alternatively purée briefly in a food processor.) Transfer to a large saucepan and pour in the chicken stock. Bring to the boil, cover and simmer for 30 minutes. Strain and reserve the stock.

3. Quarter the shallots, chop the garlic and chillies and grate the galangal. Heat the oil in a frying pan, add the shallots, garlic, chillies and galangal and fry for 5 minutes. Add to the stock with the coconut milk and sugar. Bring to the boil, cover and simmer for 20 minutes.

4. Stir in the chicken, marinade juices and peas. Return to the boil and simmer, uncovered, for 5-7 minutes until the chicken is tender.

5. Serve at once in warmed soup bowls, topped with the coriander and drizzled with a little sesame oil.

VARIATION

Substitute beef sirloin or fillet for the chicken. Add a few minutes before the peas to allow a slightly longer cooking time for the beef.

TECHNIQUE

Slice the chicken across the grain into thin slices.

MUSHROOM AND OMELETTE SOUP

Thai people frequently use eggs in their cooking and here an omelette is cut into pieces and stirred into a mushroom broth just before serving. I have used a selection of fresh and dried mushrooms, available from larger supermarkets and Oriental stores. Fresh oyster mushrooms are readily available but button or field mushrooms can be used instead.

SERVES 4

1.2 litres (2 pints) vegetable stock (see page 26)
15 g (½ oz) each dried black and dried shiitake mushrooms, or 25 g (1 oz) dried shiitake
300 ml (½ pint) boiling water
1 bunch spring onions, trimmed
1-2 garlic cloves, peeled
2 small green chillies, seeded
grated rind and juice of 1 lime
15 ml (1 tbsp) sunflower oil
10 ml (2 tsp) sesame oil
125 g (4 oz) oyster mushrooms
25 g (1 oz) canned bamboo shoots, drained
15 ml (1 tbsp) light soy sauce
OMELETTE
15 ml (1 tbsp) sunflower oil
2 eggs
salt and pepper

PREPARATION TIME
25 minutes
COOKING TIME
1 hour, plus stock
FREEZING
Not suitable

165 CALS PER SERVING

1. Strain the stock into a clean pan.

2. Place the dried mushrooms in a bowl, pour over the boiling water and leave to soak for 30 minutes. Strain and reserve the liquid; finely slice the shiitake and chop the black mushrooms.

3. Slice the spring onions and set aside. Roughly chop the garlic and chillies, then pound with the lime rind, using a pestle and mortar or a spice grinder, until well crushed.

4. Heat both the oils in a wok or frying pan and fry the garlic and chilli paste with the spring onions for 5 minutes until softened. Stir into the strained stock with the lime juice, soaked mushrooms and reserved liquid. Cover and simmer for 20 minutes.

5. Meanwhile, make the omelette. Heat the oil in a small frying pan. Beat the eggs with salt and pepper, then pour into the hot oil. Cook over a low heat, stirring occasionally, until the omelette is just set. Remove from the pan with a spatula and cut into thick strips or squares.

6. Add the oyster mushrooms, bamboo shoots and soy sauce to the soup and simmer for 4-5 minutes until all the mushrooms are tender. Stir in the omelette pieces and serve at once.

VARIATION

Instead of making an omelette, simply beat 2 eggs together and whisk into the just simmering soup at the end of cooking. Immediately remove from the heat.

TECHNIQUE

Cook the omelette over a low heat, stirring occasionally, until set.

THAI SEAFOOD SALAD

Perhaps the most delicious and exciting of all Thai salads is a combination of seafood tossed with a sweet and sour dressing. The flavours are wonderfully refreshing and this dish is visually stunning.

SERVES 4

20 fresh mussels in shells
8 large raw tiger prawns
225 g (8 oz) small squid
12 scallops, shelled
2 shallots, peeled
1 carrot
10 cm (4 inch) piece
  cucumber
75 g (3 oz) Chinese cabbage
2 lime leaves, shredded
30 ml (2 tbsp) chopped fresh
  coriander
15 ml (1 tbsp) chopped fresh
  mint
25 g (1 oz) dried grated
  coconut, toasted
DRESSING
2-3 small red chillies, seeded
15 ml (1 tbsp) lime juice
15 ml (1 tbsp) rice vinegar
15 ml (1 tbsp) Thai fish
  sauce
10 ml (2 tsp) sesame oil
pinch of sugar

PREPARATION TIME
45-50 minutes
COOKING TIME
About 10 minutes
FREEZING
Not suitable

245 CALS PER SERVING

1. Scrub the mussels thoroughly under cold running water and remove their beards. Discard any with damaged shells or any that remain opened when sharply tapped. Cut the heads off the prawns and peel away the shells. Make a shallow slit down the back of each prawn and remove the dark intestinal vein; rinse well. Clean the squid (see page 30), scoring the body pouches with a sharp knife, but leaving the tentacles whole. Clean the scallops (see technique) and separate the white meat from the coral if preferred; slice the white meat into rounds.

2. Place the mussels in a large saucepan with just the water clinging to the shells. Cover with a tight-fitting lid and steam for 4-5 minutes until the shells have opened. Discard any that remain closed. Drain, reserving the poaching liquid, and refresh the mussels under cold running water. Set aside.

3. Return the mussel liquid to the boil. Add the prawns and poach for 3 minutes, then add the squid and scallops and cook for a further 2-3 minutes until all the seafood is cooked. Remove with a slotted spoon and immediately refresh under cold running water. Reserve 30 ml (2 tbsp) of the poaching liquid.

4. Thinly slice the shallots and carrot. Halve, deseed and slice the cucumber. Shred the cabbage. Place the vegetables in a bowl and toss in the seafood, lime leaves, coriander and mint.

5. For the dressing, finely dice the chillies and mix with the rest of the ingredients. Add to the salad, toss well and divide between individual serving plates. Top each salad with toasted grated coconut and serve at once.

VARIATIONS

Use other types of seafood, such as clams instead of mussels, or cubes of white fish – such as cod or haddock – in place of squid and/or scallops.

TECHNIQUE

To clean the scallops, remove the dark beard-like fringe and tough greyish muscle from the side of the white meat.

CRAB SALAD

There is nothing quite like the taste of freshly cooked crab meat and this salad is the perfect way to appreciate it. If you are lucky enough to obtain fresh cooked crabs you will need two, each about 1.4 kg (3 lb). The dark meat is not included in this dish but it can be frozen for future use. If fresh crab is unobtainable, use frozen white meat instead, but make sure it is well drained. As a starter, this salad serves 8.

SERVES 6

450 g (1 lb) white crab meat, fresh or frozen and thawed
6 spring onions, trimmed
30 ml (2 tbsp) chopped fresh coriander
15 ml (1 tbsp) chopped fresh chives
pinch of cayenne pepper
2 garlic cloves, peeled
2.5 cm (1 inch) piece fresh root ginger, peeled
30 ml (2 tbsp) sunflower oil
2 lime leaves, shredded
2.5 ml ($\frac{1}{2}$ tsp) dried crushed chilli flakes
60 ml (4 tbsp) lime juice
15 ml (1 tbsp) sugar
5 ml (1 tsp) shrimp paste (optional)
15 ml (1 tbsp) Thai fish sauce or soy sauce
1-2 heads of radicchio or red chicory
50 g (2 oz) cucumber
25 g (1 oz) bean sprouts
TO GARNISH
lime wedges
coriander sprigs

PREPARATION TIME
20 minutes, plus crab if necessary
COOKING TIME 3 minutes
FREEZING Not suitable

165 CALS PER SERVING

1. Flake the white crab meat into shreds and place in a bowl. Finely chop the spring onions and add to the crab with the coriander, chives and cayenne pepper. Mix gently, then cover and chill until required.

2. Crush the garlic and ginger together, using a pestle and mortar or spice grinder. Heat the oil in a small pan, add the garlic, ginger, lime leaves and chilli flakes and fry over a gentle heat for 3 minutes until softened but not brown. Add the lime juice, sugar, shrimp paste if using, and the fish sauce. Stir well, then remove from the heat. Leave until cold.

3. Drizzle the cooled dressing over the crab mixture and toss lightly until evenly combined. Arrange the radicchio or chicory leaves on serving plates and spoon in the crab mixture. Thinly slice the cucumber and arrange on top of each serving with the bean sprouts. Garnish with lime wedges and coriander sprigs to serve.

NOTE: If you are unsure of preparing fresh crab yourself then ask your fishmonger to do it for you, or at least to separate the body from its shell and pull off the legs and claws. Remember to discard the stomach sac and inedible feathery gills or 'dead man's fingers'.

TECHNIQUE

If preparing the crab yourself, crack open the claws and legs and use a skewer to pick out all the meat.

BEEF SALAD WITH ROASTED VEGETABLE PASTE

This recipe is based on a Thai dish called *larp* which is similar to beef tartare. Here the beef is seared as a whole fillet, then sliced and served on a bed of tangy salad leaves. The dressing is a sweet/sour paste made from roasted vegetables; it has a distinctive Thai flavour that provides the perfect complement.

SERVES 4

225 g (8 oz) fillet steak
15 ml (1 tbsp) Szechuan
   peppercorns
5 ml (1 tsp) ground black
   pepper
5 ml (1 tsp) ground coriander
1.25 ml (¼ tsp) Chinese
   five-spice powder

VEGETABLE PASTE

225 g (8 oz) shallots, peeled
4-8 garlic cloves, peeled
2-3 large chillies, seeded
2.5 cm (1 inch) piece fresh
   root ginger, peeled
1 lemon grass stalk
5 ml (1 tsp) cumin seeds
45 ml (3 tbsp) sunflower oil
15 ml (1 tbsp) tamarind
   paste (see page 8)
15 ml (1 tbsp) light soy
   sauce or Thai fish sauce
10 ml (2 tsp) sugar

TO SERVE

125 g (4 oz) salad leaves
15 ml (1 tbsp) sesame seeds
lime wedges

PREPARATION TIME 35 minutes,
plus marinating
COOKING TIME 30-35 minutes
FREEZING Not suitable

230 CALS PER SERVING

1. Preheat the oven to 200°C (400°F) Mark 6. Wash and dry the beef. Roughly grind the Szechuan peppercorns, using a pestle and mortar or spice grinder, and mix with the black pepper, ground coriander and five-spice powder. Spread on a board. Press the steak down into the spice mixture, turning to coat well on both sides. Cover and set aside for 2 hours.

2. Meanwhile, prepare the vegetable paste. Halve any large shallots; roughly chop the garlic, chillies and ginger; finely chop the lemon grass. Place these ingredients in a small roasting pan with the cumin seeds. Pour over the oil and toss well until evenly combined. Transfer to the oven and roast for 30 minutes until browned and softened. Allow to cool slightly.

3. Transfer the roasted vegetables to a food processor and add the tamarind paste, soy sauce or fish sauce, and the sugar. Purée to form a rough paste, adding a little water if too thick. Taste and add a little salt if necessary.

4. Brush a griddle or heavy-based frying pan with a little oil and heat. As soon as the oil starts to smoke, add the beef fillet and sear by pressing down hard with a fish slice. Fry for 1 minute, turn the steak

and repeat with the second side. Remove from the pan and leave to rest for 2 minutes.

5. Divide the salad leaves between individual serving plates. Thinly slice the beef fillet and arrange on the plates. Spoon on a little of the roasted vegetable paste and scatter over the sesame seeds. Serve at once, with lime wedges.

VARIATION

Replace the fillet steak with very fresh tuna steak.

TECHNIQUE

Place the beef on a hot oiled griddle, press down firmly with a fish slice and cook for 1 minute on each side to sear.

HOT AND SOUR NOODLE AND VEGETABLE SALAD

For this tempting salad, transparent rice vermicelli noodles are tossed in a spicy lime dressing, together with a colourful selection of crispy fried vegetables. Serve the salad warm, or slightly chilled if preferred.

SERVES 4

2 carrots
50 g (2 oz) baby sweetcorn
50 g (2 oz) mangetout
50 g (2 oz) broccoli florets
1 small red pepper, seeded
125 g (4 oz) Chinese
   cabbage or pak choi
50 g (2 oz) canned water
   chestnuts, drained
30 ml (2 tbsp) peanut or
   sunflower oil
15 ml (1 tbsp) sesame oil
2 garlic cloves, crushed
5 ml (1 tsp) dried crushed
   chilli flakes
5 ml (1 tsp) grated fresh
   root ginger
75 g (3 oz) rice vermicelli
   noodles
30 ml (2 tbsp) chopped fresh
   coriander

DRESSING

30 ml (2 tbsp) peanut oil
5 ml (1 tsp) chilli oil
10 ml (2 tsp) caster sugar
30 ml (2 tbsp) lime juice
15 ml (1 tbsp) rice vinegar
15 ml (1 tbsp) Thai fish
   sauce
salt and pepper

TO GARNISH

25 g (1 oz) raw peanuts,
   toasted and chopped

PREPARATION TIME 30 minutes,
plus optional chilling
COOKING TIME 3-4 minutes
FREEZING Not suitable

345 CALS PER SERVING

1. Start by preparing the vegetables. Cut the carrots into matchsticks; halve the baby sweetcorn lengthways if large; top and tail the mangetout; cut the broccoli into small florets. Thinly slice the red pepper; roughly shred the Chinese cabbage or pak choi and slice the water chestnuts. Set aside.

2. Place the two oils in a small pan, add the garlic, chilli flakes and ginger and heat until smoking. Strain the oil into a wok or large frying pan. Add the prepared vegetables and stir-fry for 2-3 minutes until just starting to wilt. Immediately remove the pan from the heat.

3. Soak the noodles according to the packet instructions. Meanwhile, whisk all the dressing ingredients together, seasoning with salt and pepper to taste. Strain the cooked noodles and toss with a little of the dressing.

4. Stir the remaining dressing into the vegetables together with the chopped coriander. Arrange the noodles and vegetables on individual serving plates.

Scatter over the toasted peanuts and serve at once or chill for up to 1 hour before serving.

VARIATION

Include some deep-fried tofu. Cut 125 g (4 oz) plain tofu into cubes and dry well. Deep-fry in hot oil for 2-3 minutes until crisp and golden. Add to the vegetables and noodles just before serving.

TECHNIQUE

Stir-fry the vegetables in the flavoured oil for 2-3 minutes until they are just starting to wilt.

SPICY GRILLED AUBERGINE SALAD

For this unusual salad baby aubergine slices are brushed with a sweet soy glaze, then grilled until charred and tender and tossed with green beans in a sesame and lime dressing. Serve the salad while it is still warm, on a bed of lettuce leaves.

SERVES 4

4 baby aubergines, or 2 small
  ones
10 ml (2 tsp) sea salt
30 ml (2 tbsp) sweet soy
  sauce
10 ml (2 tsp) Thai fish sauce
5 ml (1 tsp) hot chilli sauce
5 ml (1 tsp) lemon juice
2.5 ml (½ tsp) ground cumin
2.5 ml (½ tsp) clear honey
125 g (4 oz) yard-long green
  beans, or French beans
1 quantity prawn paste
  (see page 22)
DRESSING
15 ml (1 tbsp) peanut or
  sunflower oil
5 ml (1 tsp) sesame oil
15 ml (1 tbsp) lime juice
pinch of sugar
TO SERVE
½ lettuce
30 ml (2 tbsp) lime juice
sesame seeds
mint leaves

PREPARATION TIME
25 minutes, plus standing
COOKING TIME
8-10 minutes
FREEZING Not suitable

100 CALS PER SERVING

1. Trim the aubergines and halve baby ones lengthways; cut small ones into 4 slices. Place the aubergines in a colander set over a plate and sprinkle over the salt. Leave to degorge the bitter juices for 30 minutes.

2. Meanwhile, in a small bowl mix together the sweet soy sauce, fish sauce, chilli sauce, lemon juice, cumin and honey. Set aside.

3. Top and tail the beans and cut into 5 cm (2 inch) lengths. Bring a large pan of lightly salted water to a rolling boil, plunge in the green beans, return to the boil and cook for 3 minutes until the beans are tender. Immediately drain and refresh the beans under cold running water. Drain again and toss with the prawn paste.

4. Preheat the grill. Rinse the aubergines to remove the salt and pat dry. Place on a rack over the grill pan and brush with the soy sauce mixture. Grill as close to the heat as possible for 2-3 minutes. Turn the slices over, brush with the remaining soy mixture and grill until charred and tender.

5. Whisk the ingredients for the dressing together until evenly blended. Toss the green beans with half of the dressing.

6. Tear the lettuce into bite-sized pieces, toss with the lime juice and arrange on individual serving plates. Top with the aubergine slices and beans, then drizzle over the remaining dressing. Scatter over the sesame seeds and mint leaves and serve at once.

NOTE: The sweet soy glaze is excellent for brushing onto fish steaks, such as salmon, to keep them moist and succulent during grilling.

TECHNIQUE

Put the aubergines in a colander set over a plate and sprinkle with the salt. Leave to degorge the bitter juices for 30 minutes.

STEAMED SEA BASS WITH COCONUT AND MANGO

For this special occasion dish, sea bass is coated with a spicy paste and steamed inside a foil parcel in the oven. This is a fine method for steaming whole fish and dispenses with the need for a large steamer or fish kettle. The aroma that pervades the air as you open the foil parcel is truly wonderful!

SERVES 4

1 sea bass, about 900 g
   (2 lb), scaled and gutted
225 g (8 oz) Savoy cabbage
4 kaffir lime leaves
2 lemon grass stalks
4 star anise
1 small firm mango
SPICE PASTE
3 shallots, peeled
2 garlic cloves, peeled
2-4 dried red chillies, seeded
4 coriander roots, scrubbed
2.5 cm (1 inch) piece
   galangal, peeled
15 ml (1 tbsp) tamarind
   paste (see page 8)
2.5 ml (½ tsp) ground black
   pepper
COCONUT SAUCE
30 ml (2 tbsp) dried shrimp
   (optional)
10 ml (2 tsp) hot chilli sauce
30 ml (2 tbsp) Thai fish sauce
30 ml (2 tbsp) rice vinegar
22.5 ml (1½ tbsp) dark
   muscovado
250 ml (8 fl oz) coconut milk
TO GARNISH
coriander sprigs
lime wedges

PREPARATION TIME 20 minutes, plus marinating
COOKING TIME 25 minutes
FREEZING Not suitable

385 CALS PER SERVING

1. Wash and dry the fish, then using a sharp knife, cut 4 deep slashes in each side of the fish.

2. To make the spice paste, roughly chop the shallots, garlic, chillies, coriander roots and galangal. Grind to a fairly smooth paste, using a spice grinder or pestle and mortar. Stir in the tamarind paste and pepper. Spread the spice paste inside the cavity and all over the surface of the fish. Place in a non-reactive dish, cover and leave to marinate for at least 4 hours, preferably overnight.

3. Preheat the oven to 220°C (425°F) Mark 7. Finely shred the cabbage, discarding the core, and arrange in a band down the middle of a large double layer of foil. Sit the fish on top. Lightly bruise the lime leaves, lemon grass and star anise, then place inside the fish cavity. Turn up the sides and ends of the foil but do not seal.

4. To prepare the coconut sauce, mince the dried shrimp if using, with a spice grinder or pestle and mortar.

Place all the sauce ingredients in a small bowl and stir well, then pour over the fish. Bring the edges of the foil over the fish and fold tightly together to seal the parcel. Place on a large baking sheet and bake in the oven for 25 minutes.

5. Remove the parcel from the oven and leave to stand for 5 minutes. Meanwhile, peel and stone the mango, then slice the flesh. Transfer the fish to a warmed serving platter with the cabbage and juices. Arrange the mango slices on top of the fish, scatter over the coriander and serve at once, with lime wedges.

VARIATIONS

Use a less expensive fish, such as salmon, grey mullet or sea trout.

TECHNIQUE

Spread the spice paste inside the fish cavity and all over the skin.

SQUID AND VEGETABLES IN A BLACK BEAN SAUCE

Don't be put off by the rather lengthy preparation time for this dish as it's quite delicious and has a particularly authentic flavour. Remember the great thing about Thai meals is that most of the preparation can be done ahead of time, and the cooking times are wonderfully short.

SERVES 4

900 g (2 lb) squid, cleaned
   (see note)
50 g (2 oz) broccoli florets
50 g (2 oz) mangetout
50 g (2 oz) carrots, peeled
75 g (3 oz) cauliflower
1 small green or red pepper,
   seeded
50 g (2 oz) Chinese cabbage
   or pak choi
25 g (1 oz) bean sprouts
30 ml (2 tbsp) sunflower oil
15 ml (1 tbsp) sesame oil
2 garlic cloves, peeled
2 dried red chillies
SAUCE
30 ml (2 tbsp) black bean
   sauce
15 ml (1 tbsp) Thai fish
   sauce
10-15 ml (2-3 tsp) clear
   honey
90 ml (3 fl oz) fish or
   vegetable stock
15 ml (1 tbsp) tamarind
   paste (see page 8)
10 ml (2 tsp) cornflour
TO GARNISH
30 ml (2 tbsp) toasted
   sesame seeds
30 ml (2 tbsp) roughly torn
   coriander

PREPARATION TIME 55 minutes
COOKING TIME 10-15 minutes
FREEZING Not suitable

360 CALS PER SERVING

1. First prepare the sauce. In a small bowl, mix together the black bean sauce, fish sauce, honey and stock. Add the tamarind paste and cornflour and whisk until smooth. Set aside.

2. Wash and dry the cleaned squid, and halve the tentacles if large. Open out the body pouches, score diagonally, then cut into large squares; set aside.

3. Prepare the vegetables. Cut the broccoli into small florets; top and tail the mangetout; peel and thinly slice the carrots; cut the cauliflower into small florets; thinly slice the green or red pepper; roughly shred the Chinese cabbage or pak choi; wash and dry the bean sprouts.

4. Heat the two oils together in a large wok or frying pan, add the garlic and whole chillies and fry gently for 5 minutes. Remove the garlic and chillies with a slotted spoon and discard.

5. Add the vegetables to the oil and stir-fry for 3 minutes. Then add the squid, increase the heat and stir-fry for a

further 2 minutes until the squid curls up and turns opaque. Add the sauce and allow to simmer for 1 minute. Scatter over the sesame seeds and coriander and serve at once.

NOTE: Refer to the instructions on page 30 for cleaning squid. Alternatively you can buy ready cleaned and prepared squid from the fish counters of some larger supermarkets; in this case you will need 500 g (1 lb 2 oz) prepared weight.

TECHNIQUE

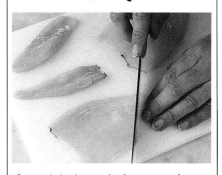

Cut each body pouch along one side and open out flat, with the inside turned uppermost. Using a sharp knife, score the flesh diagonally, without cutting all the way through.

GRILLED SPICED CHICKEN

Use large chicken breast quarters with the wing attached for this dish. Spear each one with bamboo skewers, to make it easier to turn the chicken during grilling. This is a perfect dish for cooking over a barbecue when the weather permits; note that you may need to reduce the cooking time slightly and turn and baste the chicken more frequently during barbecuing.

SERVES 4

4 large chicken breast quarters, each about 300 g (10 oz)
SPICE PASTE
15 ml (1 tbsp) sunflower oil
10 ml (2 tsp) sesame oil
2 large thin red chillies, seeded
2 garlic cloves, crushed
5 ml (1 tsp) cumin seeds
5 ml (1 tsp) fennel seeds
15 ml (1 tbsp) chopped fresh basil
5 ml (1 tsp) turmeric
15 ml (1 tbsp) dark brown sugar
30 ml (2 tbsp) rice or wine vinegar
30 ml (2 tbsp) tomato purée
2.5 ml (½ tsp) salt
TOMATO AND SHALLOT CHUTNEY
225 g (8 oz) shallots, peeled
1 garlic clove, peeled
30 ml (2 tbsp) sunflower oil
75 ml (3 fl oz) rice vinegar or wine vinegar
30 ml (2 tbsp) rice wine or dry sherry
50 g (2 oz) caster sugar
175 g (6 oz) firm cherry tomatoes
30 ml (2 tbsp) sweet soy sauce

TO SERVE
coriander sprigs
lemon wedges

PREPARATION TIME
40 minutes, plus marinating
COOKING TIME 30-35 minutes
FREEZING Not suitable

440 CALS PER SERVING

1. Start by making the spice paste. Heat the two oils together in a small pan. Chop the chillies and stir into the pan with the garlic, cumin, fennel, basil and turmeric, and fry gently for 5 minutes. Add the remaining ingredients and stir until the sugar is dissolved. Remove from the heat and leave to cool.

2. Wash and dry the chicken and, using a sharp knife, cut a few deep slashes on both sides of each quarter. Spread the spice paste over the chicken and place in a shallow, non-reactive dish. Cover and leave to marinate in a cool place for at least 4 hours, preferably overnight.

3. Make the tomato and shallot chutney. Halve any large shallots and chop the garlic. Heat the oil in a saucepan, add the shallots and garlic, and fry gently for 15 minutes until golden. Carefully add the vinegar, rice wine or sherry, sugar and 60 ml (2 fl oz) water. Bring the mixture to the boil and boil steadily over a high heat for 10 minutes.

4. Halve the cherry tomatoes and add to the pan with the soy sauce. Simmer for a further 5-10 minutes until the tomatoes are softened and the liquid reduced. Leave to cool.

5. Preheat the grill. Spear each chicken quarter with two skewers. Transfer to the grill pan and grill a good few inches below the heat for 15-20 minutes on each side, basting frequently until the chicken is cooked all the way through. Return to the grill and cook further, if at all still pink. Serve the chicken garnished with coriander and accompanied by the tomato and shallot chutney and lemon wedges.

VARIATION

Cook the marinated chicken in a preheated oven at 220°C (425°F) Mark 7 for 30-35 minutes.

TECHNIQUE

Spear the marinated chicken quarters crosswise with bamboo skewers.

GREEN CHICKEN CURRY

This dish – along with the Thai red curry – are perhaps the most famous of all Thai main meals. A basic spice paste mixture forms the basis of every curry; this is often made up in larger quantities and stored in the refrigerator for future use. The colour of the curry paste depends on the chillies used – either green as here, or red. Reduce the amount of chillies for a milder flavour.

SERVES 4

4 baby aubergines (see note)

5 ml (1 tsp) sea salt

4 shallots, peeled

2 garlic cloves, peeled

30 ml (2 tbsp) sunflower oil

30 ml (2 tbsp) green curry paste (see page 9)

150 ml (¼ pint) chicken stock

15 ml (1 tbsp) Thai fish sauce

15 ml (1 tbsp) lemon juice

350 g (12 oz) skinless chicken breast fillets

1 red pepper, seeded

125 g (4 oz) French beans, trimmed

25 g (1 oz) creamed coconut

12 deep-fried basil leaves (see page 30), to garnish (optional)

PREPARATION TIME
30 minutes, plus standing
COOKING TIME
30 minutes
FREEZING
Not suitable

255 CALS PER SERVING

1. Quarter the aubergines and sprinkle over the salt. Place in a colander set over a plate and leave to degorge the bitter juices for 30 minutes. Rinse the aubergines thoroughly to remove the salt and pat dry.

2. Halve or quarter the shallots if large and slice the garlic. Heat the oil in a large deep frying pan and fry the shallots and garlic for 3 minutes until lightly browned. Add the green curry paste and stir-fry for 2-3 minutes.

3. Carefully stir in the stock, fish sauce and lemon juice. Bring to the boil and simmer, uncovered, for 10 minutes.

4. Meanwhile, cut the chicken breast into 3 cm (1¼ inch) cubes. Slice the red pepper and halve the French beans. Add to the sauce with the aubergines and return to the boil. Simmer for 10-15 minutes until the vegetables and chicken are tender.

5. Add the creamed coconut and stir until melted and the sauce is thickened; do not reboil. Divide between warmed serving bowls and garnish with fried basil leaves, if preferred. Serve at once, with rice to accompany.

NOTE: If baby aubergines are unobtainable, use 1 small aubergine, halved and cut into wedges instead.

If you are short on time, use ready-made Thai green curry paste, available from larger supermarkets, Oriental stores and by mail order.

TECHNIQUE

Add the Thai green curry paste to the browned shallots and garlic, and stir-fry for 2-3 minutes.

DUCK BREASTS WITH PICKLED PLUMS

This dish is not a classic, although they do cook duck in Thailand. Here duck breasts are marinated, then quickly seared to seal in the flavour and finally cooked through in a rich sauce. Home-pickled plums provide a nice sharp contrast to the richness of the duck and its sauce.

SERVES 6

225 g (8 oz) duck breast
  fillets
15 ml (1 tbsp) sunflower oil
150 ml (¼ pint) chicken
  stock
30 ml (2 tbsp) oyster sauce
MARINADE
2 garlic cloves, crushed
5 ml (1 tsp) hot chilli sauce
pinch of salt
10 ml (2 tsp) clear honey
10 ml (2 tsp) dark
  muscovado sugar
30 ml (2 tbsp) lime juice
15 ml (1 tbsp) dark soy
  sauce
PICKLED PLUMS
6 large under-ripe plums
50 g (2 oz) caster sugar
50 ml (2 fl oz) distilled malt
  vinegar
1.25 ml (¼ tsp) dried
  crushed chilli flakes
5 ml (1 tsp) salt
pinch of ground cinnamon

PREPARATION TIME
15 minutes, plus marinating
COOKING TIME
15 minutes
FREEZING Not suitable

335 CALS PER SERVING

1. First mix together all of the ingredients for the marinade. Skin the duck breasts, wash well and dry thoroughly. Cut a few deep slashes in each duck breast and place in a shallow, non-reactive dish. Spread evenly with the marinade, then cover and leave to marinate for at least 4 hours, turning the duck breasts several times.

2. Meanwhile, prepare the pickled plums. Wash and dry the plums, halve and remove the stones. Place the remaining ingredients in a saucepan with 50 ml (2 fl oz) water and heat gently, stirring until the sugar is dissolved. Add the plums, bring to the boil and simmer gently for 5 minutes or until the plums have just softened. Set aside to cool.

3. When ready to serve, remove the duck breasts from the marinade and pat dry, reserving the marinade juices. Heat the oil in a large non-stick frying pan and brown the duck quickly on both sides. Add the stock, marinade juices and oyster sauce and simmer gently, covered, for 5 minutes. Remove the duck breasts with a slotted spoon and keep warm.

4. Remove the plums from their liquid with a slotted spoon and carefully add to the duck sauce. Bring to the boil and simmer, uncovered, for a further 5 minutes. Slice the duck breasts and arrange on warmed serving plates with the plum halves. Spoon over the sauce and serve at once, with rice or noodles.

VARIATION

Replace the plums with 6 small oranges, peel and pith removed.

TECHNIQUE

Slash the duck breasts using a sharp knife, to allow the marinade to permeate through the meat.

SPICED BEEF AND COCONUT CURRY

The combination of different spices gives this robust curry its distinctive flavour. Beef, potatoes, onions and chillies are simmered in a spiced coconut broth, and cashew nuts are added to the stew just before serving. Accompany the curry with plain boiled Thai rice.

SERVES 4

450 g (1 lb) sirloin steak
4 cloves
5 ml (1 tsp) coriander seeds
5 ml (1 tsp) cumin seeds
seeds from 3 cardamom pods
2 garlic cloves, peeled
2.5 cm (1 inch) piece fresh
   root ginger, peeled
1 small onion, peeled
30 ml (2 tbsp) sunflower oil
15 ml (1 tbsp) sesame oil
15 ml (1 tbsp) Indian curry
   paste
5 ml (1 tsp) turmeric
225 g (8 oz) potatoes,
   peeled
4 tomatoes
5 ml (1 tsp) sugar
15 ml (1 tbsp) light soy sauce
300 ml (½ pint) coconut milk
150 ml (¼ pint) beef or
   chicken stock
4 fresh red chillies, bruised
50 g (2 oz) cashew nuts

PREPARATION TIME
30 minutes
COOKING TIME
40-45 minutes
FREEZING
Not suitable

505 CALS PER SERVING

1. Cut the steak into 3 cm (1¼ inch) cubes.

2. Place the cloves and coriander, cumin and cardamom seeds in a small heavy-based frying pan. Roast over a high heat for 1-2 minutes until the spices are golden and release their aroma. Cool slightly, then grind to a powder in a spice grinder or blender.

3. Roughly chop the garlic, ginger and onion, then purée in a food processor to form a smooth paste. Heat the two oils together in a deep frying pan. Add the onion purée with the curry paste and stir-fry for 5 minutes, then add the roasted ground spices and turmeric and fry for a further 5 minutes.

4. Add the beef to the pan and fry for a further 5 minutes until browned on all sides. Quarter the potatoes and tomatoes and add to the pan with all the remaining ingredients, except the cashews. Bring to the boil, lower the heat and simmer, covered, for 20-25 minutes until the beef is tender and the potatoes are cooked.

5. Stir in the cashew nuts and serve the curry with plain boiled rice or noodles and stir-fried vegetables.

VARIATION

For a vegetable curry, replace the steak with 450 g (1 lb) of your favourite root vegetables. Celeriac and sweet potato, for example, make a particularly delicious combination. Add to the sauce along with the potatoes and cook for 25-30 minutes until tender.

TECHNIQUE

Dry roast the whole spices in a small heavy-based pan until they release their aroma.

LAMB AND BAMBOO SHOOT RED CURRY

This recipe includes the classic Thai red curry paste which is used so extensively in Thai cooking. It is quick and easy to make and often only a little is needed to give heat and flavour; the rest can be stored in a sealed jar in the refrigerator for up to 1 week. Commercial red curry pastes are available from many larger supermarkets as well as Oriental stores and by mail order.

SERVES 4

1 large onion, peeled
2 garlic cloves, peeled
450 g (1 lb) lean lamb
30 ml (2 tbsp) sunflower oil
30 ml (2 tbsp) Thai red
  curry paste (see page 8)
150 ml (¼ pint) lamb or
  beef stock
30 ml (2 tbsp) Thai fish
  sauce
10 ml (2 tsp) soft brown
  sugar
200 g (7 oz) can bamboo
  shoots, drained
1 red pepper, seeded
30 ml (2 tbsp) chopped fresh
  mint
15 ml (1 tbsp) chopped fresh
  basil
25 g (1 oz) raw peanuts,
  toasted
basil leaves, to garnish

PREPARATION TIME
30 minutes
COOKING TIME
45 minutes
FREEZING
Not suitable

325 CALS PER SERVING

1. Cut the onion into wedges and finely chop the garlic. Cut the lamb into 3 cm (1¼ inch) cubes. Heat the oil in a wok or large frying pan, add the onion and garlic and fry over a medium heat for 5 minutes.

2. Add the lamb together with the curry paste and stir-fry for 5 minutes. Add the stock, fish sauce and sugar. Bring to the boil, lower the heat, cover and simmer gently for 20 minutes.

3. Meanwhile, slice the bamboo shoots and red pepper. Stir into the curry with the herbs and cook, uncovered, for a further 10 minutes. Stir in the peanuts and serve at once, garnished with the basil leaves.

VARIATION

For a Thai-style Sunday roast, spread a layer of red curry paste over a leg of lamb before roasting on a bed of garlic, shallots, ginger, lime leaves, chillies and lemon grass. Strain off the cooking juices into a small pan, whisk in a little coconut milk and bring to the boil. Serve this sauce with the lamb and vegetables.

TECHNIQUE

Add the lamb to the wok with the curry paste and stir-fry for 5 minutes.

STUFFED THAI OMELETTE

This is a great supper dish for vegetarians, combining classic ingredients from several different countries and continents. I have adapted an Italian-style pesto by substituting coriander for basil and adding a few Thai flavourings. Stir-fried vegetables are tossed with this pesto to make a delicious stuffing for the omelette.

SERVES 2

50 g (2 oz) aubergine
50 g (2 oz) shiitake or
   button mushrooms
1/2 small red pepper, seeded
50 g (2 oz) French beans
2 spring onions, trimmed
25 g (1 oz) shelled peas,
   thawed if frozen
45 ml (3 tbsp) sunflower oil
6 eggs
CORIANDER PESTO
1 shallot, peeled
1 garlic clove, peeled
1/2 small red chilli, seeded
1 coriander root, scrubbed
15 g (1/2 oz) coriander leaves
pinch of caster sugar
10 ml (2 tsp) light soy sauce
15 ml (1 tbsp) sunflower oil
salt and pepper
TO SERVE
light soy sauce

PREPARATION TIME
20 minutes
COOKING TIME
10-12 minutes
FREEZING
Not suitable

650 CALS PER SERVING

1. Start by making the coriander pesto. Roughly chop the shallot, garlic, chilli and coriander root, then grind to a fairly smooth paste with all the remaining ingredients, using a spice grinder or pestle and mortar. Season to taste and set aside.

2. Prepare the vegetables. Dice the aubergine; thinly slice the mushrooms and red pepper; trim and slice the beans; thickly slice the spring onions and pat frozen peas dry.

3. Heat 15 ml (1 tbsp) oil in a wok or frying pan, add the aubergines and fry, stirring, over a high heat for 3-4 minutes until golden. Add the remaining vegetables, except frozen peas, and stir-fry for 3-4 minutes until tender. (Add frozen peas for the last 30 seconds.) Remove from heat and stir in the pesto to taste.

4. Beat the eggs together in a bowl and season with salt and pepper to taste. Heat the remaining 30 ml (2 tbsp) oil in a large non-stick frying pan, tip in the egg mixture and swirl to the edges of the pan. Cook the omelette until it is set and browned underneath, but still slightly runny on top.

5. Spoon the vegetable mixture onto one half of the omelette, carefully flip the other half over the top and cook over a low heat for a few more minutes until set and the vegetables are heated through. Serve at once, accompanied by light soy sauce.

VARIATION

Slice 125 g (4 oz) skinless chicken breast fillet and stir-fry with the aubergine.

TECHNIQUE

Swirl the egg mixture over the base of the frying pan and cook until the omelette is set and browned underneath.

GINGERED PRAWNS WITH COCONUT RICE

This rich aromatic rice dish is substantial enough to provide a meal in itself. The coconut rice is cooked separately from the delicious stir-fried gingered prawns, which are stirred in at the end and allowed to sit undisturbed for a few minutes so the flavours can mingle. The papaya adds a striking freshness. A simple green salad is an ideal accompaniment.

SERVES 4

225 g (8 oz) long-grain rice
25 g (1 oz) butter
3 cardamom pods, bruised
250 ml (8 fl oz) coconut milk
5 ml (1 tsp) sea salt
5 ml (1 tsp) caster sugar
4 kaffir lime leaves, bruised
450 g (1 lb) raw tiger prawns
2 garlic cloves, peeled
5 cm (2 inch) piece fresh
    root ginger, peeled
30 ml (2 tbsp) sunflower oil
2.5 ml (½ tsp) dried crushed
    chilli flakes
1 small papaya
15 g (½ oz) dried grated or
    shredded coconut,
    toasted
30 ml (2 tbsp) lime or lemon
    juice

PREPARATION TIME
25 minutes, plus soaking
COOKING TIME
20-25 minutes
FREEZING
Not suitable

565 CALS PER SERVING

1. Soak the rice in cold water to cover for 1 hour, then drain well. Melt the butter in a saucepan, add the rice and cardamom pods and stir over a medium heat for 1 minute until all the grains are glossy.

2. Stir in the coconut milk, salt, sugar, lime leaves and 250 ml (8 fl oz) of water. Bring to the boil, lower the heat and simmer gently, uncovered, for 10 minutes. Cover the pan with a layer of foil, then position the lid to ensure a tight seal. Place over a *very* low heat for 10-12 minutes.

3. Meanwhile, prepare the prawns. Remove the heads and peel away the shells, then make a slit down the back of each one and remove the black intestinal vein. Wash well and pat dry; set aside.

4. Finely chop the garlic and thinly shred the ginger. Heat the oil in a wok, add the garlic, ginger and chilli flakes and stir-fry for 1 minute. Add the prawns and stir-fry for a further 5 minutes. Remove the pan from the heat and carefully stir in the cooked coconut rice until evenly combined. Cover and set aside.

5. Peel the papaya, cut in half and discard the seeds. Slice the flesh thinly.

6. Transfer the rice and prawns to a warmed serving plate, arrange the sliced papaya over the top, scatter over the toasted coconut and drizzle with the lime juice. Serve at once.

VARIATION

If raw prawns are unobtainable, use large cooked shelled ones instead, but stir-fry them for 1 minute only before adding the rice. Remove the heads from the prawns and peel away the shells, leaving on the pretty tail shells if preferred.

TECHNIQUE

Remove the heads from the prawns and peel away the shells. If preferred, leave on tail shells for a decorative effect.

RICE WITH ASPARAGUS, CRAB AND PINEAPPLE

In this exotic rice dish, cooked rice is tossed with stir-fried vegetables and spices, and heated through. The combination of flavours is exciting and delicious and that typical sweet/sour taste so inherent of Thai dishes is provided by the fresh pineapple.

SERVES 4

2 fresh small green chillies, seeded

2 garlic cloves, peeled

4 spring onions, trimmed

225 g (8 oz) thin asparagus spears, trimmed

125 g (4 oz) fresh pineapple slices

30 ml (2 tbsp) sunflower oil

5 ml (1 tsp) paprika

2.5 ml (½ tsp) ground coriander

1.25 ml (¼ tsp) cayenne pepper

225 g (8 oz) cooked Thai fragrant rice (see page 7)

150 g (5 oz) white crab meat, fresh or frozen and thawed

2 eggs, beaten

15 ml (1 tbsp) Thai fish sauce

15 ml (1 tbsp) lime juice

salt and pepper

lime wedges, to serve

PREPARATION TIME
30 minutes
COOKING TIME
15 minutes, plus the rice
FREEZING
Not suitable

390 CALS PER SERVING

1. Finely chop the chillies, garlic and spring onions; cut the asparagus spears into short lengths. Remove the core from the pineapple slices and cut into chunks.

2. Heat the oil in a wok, add the chillies, garlic, spring onions and spices and fry over a low heat for 5 minutes. Increase the heat and add the asparagus. Stir-fry for 2 minutes, then add the rice and crab meat and stir-fry for a further 2-3 minutes.

3. Add the eggs to the pan and stir over a high heat for 2-3 minutes until just set. Add the pineapple chunks, fish sauce and lime juice. Cover and heat through for 5 minutes. Season with salt and pepper to taste. Serve at once, with the lime wedges.

NOTE: When possible buy fresh crab meat from your fishmonger or super-market fresh fish counter; alternatively buy freshly frozen meat. Both of these are superior to canned crab meat which should only be used as a last resort.

TECHNIQUE

Add the beaten eggs to the pan and stir over a high heat for 2-3 minutes until just set.

STIR-FRIED BEEF WITH NOODLES AND CHILLI

For this quick noodle dish, minced beef is stir-fried with curry paste, garlic, ginger and spices, then tossed with noodles and vegetables. The curry paste used is the Indian-style paste which is widely available. If preferred, use strips of steak rather than minced beef (see variation).

SERVES 4

125 g (4 oz) dried egg thread
    noodles
1 small onion, peeled
2 garlic cloves, peeled
2.5 cm (1 inch) piece fresh
    root ginger, peeled
1 red pepper, seeded
125 g (4 oz) French beans
45 ml (3 tbsp) sunflower oil
15 ml (1 tbsp) dark soy sauce
4 kaffir lime leaves, shredded
225 g (8 oz) lean minced
    beef
30 ml (2 tbsp) Indian
    medium curry paste
5 ml (1 tsp) turmeric
2.5 ml ($\frac{1}{2}$ tsp) paprika
1.25 ml ($\frac{1}{4}$ tsp) chilli powder
SAUCE
30 ml (2 tbsp) tamarind
    paste (see page 8)
15 ml (1 tbsp) Thai fish sauce
10 ml (2 tsp) sugar
90 ml (3 fl oz) beef stock
TO GARNISH
fried basil leaves (see page 30),
    or fresh coriander leaves

PREPARATION TIME 20 minutes
COOKING TIME 15 minutes
FREEZING Not suitable

325 CALS PER SERVING

1. Soak the noodles according to the packet instructions; drain well and pat dry.

2. Meanwhile prepare the sauce. Place the tamarind paste in a bowl and whisk in the remaining ingredients until smooth. Set aside.

3. Finely chop the onion and garlic; grate the ginger. Slice the red pepper; halve the French beans.

4. Heat 15 ml (1 tbsp) of the oil in a wok or large frying pan, add the noodles and soy sauce and stir-fry for 30 seconds. Remove from the pan and set aside.

5. Add the remaining oil to the pan. Add the onion, garlic, ginger and lime leaves and fry, stirring, for 5 minutes. Add the beef, curry paste and spices and stir-fry for 3 minutes.

6. Add the red pepper and beans, and stir-fry for 3 minutes. Blend in the sauce and simmer for a further 3 minutes. Carefully stir in the noodles and heat through for 2 minutes. Transfer to a warmed serving dish. Garnish with the basil leaves or fresh coriander and serve at once.

VARIATION

Use thin strips of fillet or rump steak instead of mince. (Illustrated on cover.)

TECHNIQUE

Stir-fry the noodles with the soy sauce for 30 seconds.

THAI STIR-FRIED NOODLES WITH TOFU

This recipe is based on the classic Thai noodle dish called *phat thai* which is basically a combination of rice noodles, dried shrimp, tofu, eggs and vegetables coated in a tangy peanut sauce. This dish, or a variation of it, is typical of the noodle dishes sold as snacks from street stalls throughout Thailand.

SERVES 4

125 g (4 oz) tofu
8 shallots, peeled
1 garlic clove, peeled
2.5 cm (1 inch) piece fresh
    root ginger, peeled
30 ml (2 tbsp) sweet soy
    sauce
5 ml (1 tsp) rice vinegar
225 g (8 oz) rice noodles
30 ml (2 tbsp) sunflower oil
15 g (½ oz) dried shrimp
    (optional)
1 egg, beaten
25 g (1 oz) bean sprouts
25 g (1 oz) raw peanuts,
    chopped and toasted
SAUCE
1 dried red chilli, seeded
30 ml (2 tbsp) lemon juice
15 ml (1 tbsp) Thai fish sauce
15 ml (1 tbsp) caster sugar
30 ml (2 tbsp) smooth
    peanut butter
TO GARNISH
basil leaves

PREPARATION TIME
25 minutes
COOKING TIME 35 minutes
FREEZING Not suitable

400 CALS PER SERVING

1. Preheat the oven to 200°C (400°F) Mark 6. Drain the tofu and cut into 2.5 cm (1 inch) cubes. Halve the shallots and place in a small roasting pan with the tofu.

2. Crush the garlic and ginger and blend with the sweet soy sauce, vinegar and 30 ml (2 tbsp) water. Pour over the tofu and shallots and toss well. Roast near the top of the oven for 30 minutes until the tofu and shallots are golden.

3. Meanwhile soak the noodles according to the packet instructions. Drain, refresh under cold running water and set aside.

4. Make the sauce. Finely chop the chilli and place in a small pan with the remaining ingredients. Stir over a gentle heat until the sugar is dissolved. Keep warm.

5. Heat the oil in a wok and stir-fry the dried shrimp, if using, for 1 minute. Add the noodles and egg to the wok and stir over a medium heat for 3 minutes. Add the tofu and shallots, together with any pan juices. Stir well, then remove from the heat.

6. Stir in the bean sprouts and sauce and divide between warmed serving plates. Sprinkle with the toasted peanuts and serve at once, garnished with basil.

VARIATION

Replace the tofu with 125 g (4 oz) minced pork. Quickly stir-fry the pork, shallots, garlic and ginger in a little oil until browned. Stir in the noodles and eggs and stir-fry for 2 minutes, then add the remaining ingredients, cover the pan and heat through.

TECHNIQUE

Drain the noodles, then refresh under cold running water.

STIR-FRIED VEGETABLES WITH OYSTER SAUCE

This vibrant fresh-tasting vegetable dish can be served either as a side dish to a curry, or as a main meal with plain boiled rice or noodles. Vary the combination of vegetables according to availability and taste.

SERVES 4

175 g (6 oz) tofu

vegetable oil, for deep-frying

2 garlic cloves, peeled

1 green pepper, seeded

225 g (8 oz) broccoli

125 g (4 oz) yard-long beans
  or French beans

50 g (2 oz) bean sprouts

50 g (2 oz) canned straw
  mushrooms

125 g (4 oz) canned water
  chestnuts

30 ml (2 tbsp) vegetable oil

SAUCE

100 ml (3½ fl oz) vegetable
  stock

30 ml (2 tbsp) oyster sauce

15 ml (1 tbsp) light soy
  sauce

10 ml (2 tsp) clear honey

5 ml (1 tsp) cornflour

pinch of salt

TO GARNISH

30 ml (2 tbsp) chopped fresh
  coriander

PREPARATION TIME
30 minutes
COOKING TIME
12-15 minutes
FREEZING
Not suitable

300 CALS PER SERVING

1. Drain the tofu, dry well on kitchen paper and cut into large cubes. Heat a 10 cm (4 inch) depth of vegetable oil in a deep saucepan until it registers 180°C (350°F) on a thermometer or until a cube of bread dropped into the oil browns in 30 seconds. Add the tofu and deep-fry for 1-2 minutes until crisp and golden. Drain on kitchen paper; set aside.

2. Blend all the ingredients for the sauce together and set aside.

3. Thinly slice the garlic; slice the green pepper. Cut the broccoli into small florets and any stalk into thin slices. Trim the beans and cut into short lengths; wash and dry the bean sprouts; drain the mushrooms and water chestnuts.

4. Heat the 30 ml (2 tbsp) vegetable oil in a wok or large frying pan, add the garlic and fry for 1 minute. Carefully remove the garlic using a slotted spoon and discard. Add the green pepper, broccoli and beans, and stir-fry for 3 minutes. Add the bean sprouts, mushrooms and water chestnuts and stir-fry for 1 minute.

5. Add the tofu together with the sauce and bring to the boil. Simmer covered for 3-4 minutes until the vegetables are tender. Sprinkle with the chopped coriander and serve at once.

NOTE: Canned straw mushrooms are available from larger supermarkets and Oriental food stores. As an alternative use small fresh button mushrooms, adding them to the stir-fry 2 minutes earlier than the bean sprouts.

VARIATION

Use black bean sauce instead of oyster sauce.

TECHNIQUE

Deep-fry the cubes of tofu for 1-2 minutes until golden and crisp. Drain on kitchen paper.

EXOTIC FRESH FRUIT SALAD

Cooling, refreshing fruits are just what's required to round off a Thai meal, which is likely to have been spicy and hot. Feel free to choose your favourite fruits but, if you are serving a complete Thai dinner, try to be as authentic as possible.

SERVES 4

225 g (8 oz) wedge
 watermelon
225 g (8 oz) wedge galia or
 ogen melon
1 small papaya
1 small mango
125 g (4 oz) fresh pineapple
 slices
2 small bananas
JASMINE SYRUP
1 jasmine tea bag
2 strips lime peel
30 ml (2 tbsp) lime juice
25 g (1 oz) sugar
TO DECORATE
finely shredded lime rind
 (optional)

PREPARATION TIME
20 minutes, plus infusing
COOKING TIME
5-6 minutes
FREEZING
Not suitable

150 CALS PER SERVING

1. First make the syrup. Put the tea bag in a small bowl, pour on 150 ml (¼ pint) boiling water and leave to stand for 10 minutes. Discard the tea bag and pour the tea into a small pan. Add the lime peel, lime juice and sugar and heat gently, stirring until the sugar is dissolved. Simmer gently for 5 minutes, remove from the heat and leave to go cold.

2. Prepare the fruit. Scoop out the seeds from both melon wedges and carefully cut the flesh away from the skin. Slice the flesh and place in a large bowl.

3. Halve the papaya, scoop out and discard the seeds, then slice the flesh. Peel the mango and cut down either side of the central stone; cube the flesh. Core and quarter the pineapple slices. Peel and slice the bananas. Combine all the fruits together in a bowl.

4. Pour over the cold tea syrup and leave to marinate for 10 minutes before serving. Decorate with shredded lime rind if preferred.

VARIATIONS

Other teas, including fruit-flavoured infusions, can be substituted for the Jasmine tea – simply choose your favourite.

TECHNIQUE

Scoop the seeds from the melon then cut the flesh away from the skin, before slicing.

BANANA FRITTERS

These crisp, light fritters are totally delicious – especially if you enjoy the flavour of cooked bananas. Coconut adds flavour and texture to the coating batter, which is very simple to make. Other fruits can be used instead of bananas if you prefer (see variation).

SERVES 4-6

1 egg, separated
15 ml (1 tbsp) sunflower oil
100 ml (3½ fl oz) coconut
    milk
50 g (2 oz) plain flour
15 g (½ oz) desiccated
    coconut
25 g (1 oz) sugar
5 ml (1 tsp) ground mixed
    spice
4 large bananas
vegetable oil for deep-frying
icing sugar and ground
    cinnamon, for dusting
    (optional)

PREPARATION TIME
About 10 minutes, plus resting
COOKING TIME
About 10 minutes
FREEZING
Not suitable

465-310 CALS PER SERVING

1. Place the egg yolk in a large bowl with the oil, coconut milk, flour, coconut, sugar and mixed spice. Beat well, using a wooden spoon, to form a smooth batter. Cover and set aside for 30 minutes.

2. Peel and slice the bananas into 5 cm (2 inch) lengths. Whisk the egg white until stiff, then carefully fold into the batter until evenly combined.

3. Heat a 10 cm (4 inch) depth of vegetable oil in a deep saucepan until it registers 180°C (350°F) on a thermometer or until a cube of bread dropped into the oil browns in 30 seconds. Deep-fry the banana pieces a few at a time. Dip them into the batter to coat, then deep-fry in the hot oil for 2-3 minutes until crisp and golden.

4. Drain the fritters on kitchen paper and keep hot while cooking the remainder. Dust with icing sugar mixed with a little ground cinnamon and serve the fritters hot, accompanied by a scoop of vanilla ice cream if wished.

VARIATIONS

● Other fruits can be cooked as fritters although some work better than others: peeled, cored and thickly sliced apples, and thickly sliced peaches and nectarines work well.
● Other spices and flavourings can be added to the batter. Try adding a little grated orange rind, or replace the mixed spice with cinnamon.

TECHNIQUE

Deep-fry the battered banana slices in the hot oil for 2-3 minutes until crisp and golden. Remove with a slotted spoon and drain on kitchen paper.

MANGO, GINGER AND CITRUS SORBET

Mangoes are ideal for making sorbets as their creamy texture lends itself perfectly to the freezing process. As the flesh starts to freeze very few ice crystals form – ensuring a smooth-textured result. The sweetness of the ginger and mango is balanced by the lime juice to produce a tangy, refreshing dessert. Remember to transfer the sorbet from the freezer about 20 minutes before serving to soften slightly.

SERVES 4-6

2 large mangoes, each about
   400 g (14 oz)
25 g (1 oz) preserved stem
   ginger
50 ml (2 fl oz) syrup from
   the stem ginger jar
50 g (2 oz) caster sugar
finely pared rind and juice of
   3 limes

PREPARATION TIME
25 minutes
COOKING TIME
3-4 minutes
FREEZING TIME
5-6 hours

140-95 CALS PER SERVING

1. Peel the mangoes, using a potato peeler, then cut down either side of the central stone; cut away as much of the remaining flesh as possible. Chop the mango flesh and purée in a blender or food processor until very smooth. Transfer to a bowl and set aside. Finely chop the stem ginger and stir into the purée.

2. Place the ginger syrup in a small pan with the sugar, lime rind and juice, and add 90 ml (3 fl oz) water. Heat gently, stirring until the sugar is dissolved. Bring to the boil and simmer for 3 minutes. Remove from the heat and leave to cool.

3. Strain the cooled syrup through a fine sieve into the puréed mango mixture and stir well. Transfer to a plastic container and freeze for 2 hours. Remove from the freezer and beat well to break down any ice crystals that may have formed. Return to the freezer for a further 1 hour, then beat again. Repeat once more. Freeze for several hours until firm, or until required.

4. Transfer the sorbet to the refrigerator about 20 minutes before serving to soften slightly. Scoop into individual glass dishes to serve.

VARIATION

Mango Ice Cream: Heat 300 ml (½ pint) double cream with 2 strips lemon rind until boiling. Remove from heat and leave to infuse for 30 minutes, then strain. Whisk into 3 egg yolks, then heat gently until thickened; do not boil. Cool, then combine with the puréed flesh of 2 large mangoes and 30 ml (2 tbsp) lemon juice. Freeze in a suitable container, stirring every hour until firm.

TECHNIQUE

Beat the semi-frozen sorbet three times during freezing to break down any ice crystals which may have formed.

BAKED MOONG BEAN CUSTARD

This recipe is adapted from a similar dish I enjoyed in a Thai restaurant in London. Split mung beans are cooked until soft and then beaten with egg, sugar, coconut milk, rice flour and spices to make a batter. This is topped with grated dried coconut and baked like a cake, then served with fresh strawberries. Although not authentic it's delicious served with a drizzle of cream!

SERVES 8

140 g (4½ oz) split mung beans
150 ml (¼ pint) coconut milk
1 egg, beaten
125 g (4 oz) caster sugar
25 g (1 oz) rice flour
2.5 ml (½ tsp) ground cinnamon
pinch of grated nutmeg
15 g (½ oz) dried grated or shredded coconut
125 g (4 oz) strawberries, hulled
icing sugar, for dusting
a little single cream, to serve (optional)

PREPARATION TIME
10 minutes
COOKING TIME
1¼ hours
FREEZING
Not suitable

170 CALS PER SERVING

1. Wash the beans under cold running water until the water runs clear. Place in a saucepan and pour in enough water to cover the beans by 5 cm (2 inches). Bring slowly to the boil, cover and simmer over a low heat for 30-35 minutes until completely soft. Drain off any excess water and press the beans through a sieve to form a smooth paste. Set aside to cool.

2. Preheat the oven to 190°C (375°F) Mark 5. Grease and line a 20 cm (8 inch) cake tin. Transfer the bean purée to a large bowl and beat in the coconut milk, egg, sugar, rice flour and spices. Pour into the prepared tin and scatter the coconut over the surface.

3. Bake in the centre of the oven for 45 minutes until pale golden and firm in the centre. Leave in the tin to cool slightly. Meanwhile halve or slice the strawberries.

4. Carefully remove the warm custard cake from its tin and transfer to a serving plate. Top with the strawberries and dust with icing sugar. Serve cut into wedges, accompanied by pouring cream, if wished.

NOTE: Split mung beans are the hulled seeds of the mung bean (often called moong bean). They are pale yellow in colour and are available from Indian and ethnic stores, as well a healthfood shops and some supermarkets.

The bean purée can be prepared ahead if wished, covered closely with cling film and refrigerated overnight. Return to room temperature before adding the remaining ingredients.

TECHNIQUE

Press the cooked beans through a sieve into a bowl, to form a smooth paste.

INDEX

Thai ingredients can be obtained by mail order from:
THE STEAMBOAT FOOD AND DRINK LIMITED, P.O. Box 452, Bradford, West Yorkshire, BD4 7TF; Tel/Fax: 0274 619826
and from:- THE CURRY DIRECTORY, P.O. Box 7, Liss, Hants, GU33 7YS; Tel/Fax: 0730 894949

If you would like further information about the **Good Housekeeping Cookery Club**, please write to:
Penny Smith, Ebury Press, Random House, 20 Vauxhall Bridge Road, London SW1V 2SA.